Good Food Made Simple

SOUP

Good Food Made Simple

SOUP

*Over 140 delicious recipes, 500 color photographs,
step-by-step images, and nutritional information*

First published in 2013
LOVE FOOD is an imprint of Parragon Books Ltd

Parragon Inc.
440 Park Avenue South, 13th Floor
New York, NY 10016

www.parragon.com/lovefood

ISBN: 978-1-4723-1918-0

Printed in China

New recipes, introduction, and notes by Rachel Carter
New photography by Clive Streeter
Additional design by Geoff Borin
Edited by Fiona Biggs
Nutritional analysis by Fiona Hunter

Notes for the Reader
This book uses standard kitchen measuring spoons and cups. All spoon and cup
measurements are level unless otherwise indicated. Unless otherwise stated, milk
is assumed to be whole, butter is assumed to be salted, eggs are large, individual
vegetables are medium, and pepper is freshly ground black pepper. Unless
otherwise stated, all root vegetables should be washed and peeled before using.

For the best results, use a meat thermometer when cooking meat and poultry—
check the latest USDA government guidelines for current advice.

Garnishes and serving suggestions are all optional and not necessarily included
in the recipe ingredients or method. The times given are only an approximate
guide. Preparation times differ according to the techniques used by different
people and the cooking times may also vary from those given. Optional
ingredients, variations, or serving suggestions have not been included in the
calculations.

Recipes using raw or very lightly cooked eggs should be avoided by infants, the
elderly, pregnant women, and people with weakened immune systems. Pregnant
and breast-feeding women are advised to avoid eating peanuts and peanut
products. People with nut allergies should be aware that some of the prepared
ingredients used in the recipes in this book may contain nuts. Always check the
packaging before use.

Contents

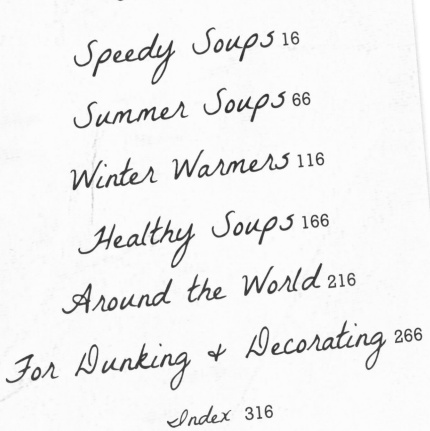

Introduction

Whether you need a comforting winter warmer, a light summer bite, or a quick and easy weeknight dinner—soup is the ideal solution to mealtime dilemmas. Easy to make, great for leftovers, and packed with nutritious ingredients, it's a filling and endlessly adaptable part of any cook's repertoire.

Few dishes are as versatile as soup: they are an economical way of using cupboard staples and leftover foods, and they are often a quick, fuss-free meal that can be made with ease. Soup can also be a simple way to include health-boosting ingredients in your diet. Packed with vegetables, and often low in saturated fat, they are a good go-to meal whether you're watching your weight or not. Plus, with the addition of grains, beans, pastas, and noodles, soup is a great way to stay fuller for longer, keeping hunger pangs at bay with these added carbohydrates.

Soups can be served as a palate cleanser before a big meal, or between courses, as a light appetizer before a rich main dish or as a substantial meal in a bowl all by itself. They are great for lunch and serve as the ideal midday energy booster.

The chapters of this book include *Speedy Soups*, which contains recipes that are ready to go in under an hour and require a minimal amount of precooking prep. *Summer Soups* includes light and refreshing recipes that use typically seasonal ingredients. This chapter also includes chilled soups, which are perfect for a hot summer's day. *Winter Warmers* include classic pureed soups containing root vegetables and squashes, which are at their best in the colder months. There are also a number of classic soup recipes that are synonymous with winter. *Healthy Soups* are ideal for anyone keeping an eye on their intake, with all the recipes being low in calories or saturated fat but still filled with ingredients to keep you satisfied until dinner. Soups from *Around The World* short lists some of the best international recipes. Finally, *Dunking and Decorating* offers a plethora of ideas for delicious baked goods ideal for serving with soups, plus crispy croutons and soup toppers that will add flavor and texture to your creations.

With minimal ingredient prep and a simple stove-top cooking process, soups are a good fuss-free meal to slot into busy lifestyles.

The Essential Staples

● Basic Vegetables

Onions, (try buying them diced and frozen, to save yourself time), garlic, and ginger (which are also available in long-life jars or frozen), celery, leeks, and carrots are all ideal for making a flavorful base for soup.

● Prepared Stock

There is a huge variety of stock options readily available from the supermarket—there are cartons and cans of liquid stock, dried bouillon cubes, packets and jars of dried stock powder, and jars of stock base. Keep a

selection in different flavors, if you can, but chicken bouillon cubes and vegetable bouillon cubes are definite pantry essentials.

● Oils

There is no need to use expensive extra virgin olive oil in soup. A basic canola, olive, or vegetable oil with a neutral flavor is preferable.

● Flavorings

Keep good-quality sea salt and whole black peppercorns, because these provide a good depth of flavor. Other basic condiments that often come in useful include balsamic vinegar, tomato paste, dark soy sauce, miso paste, mustard (French and whole-grain), ketchup, and Worcestershire sauce. There are also an increasing assortment of pastes available, and those with Parmesan and dried porcini mushrooms provide a hit of flavor that complements both vegetable- and meat-base soups.

● Beans

Whether you choose dried or canned beans, they should always be on hand because they add bulk and flavor and are both nutritious and easy on the budget. Remember that not all dried beans need to be soaked before using—split peas, red lentils, and adzuki beans can be added directly to the soup after a quick rinse in cold water. Dried red lentils can be cooked in the soup, along with other ingredients without the need for soaking, and because they are high in protein, they are ideal for

adding to vegetable soups. Keep a small selection of canned beans, such as cranberry, cannellini, red kidney beans, black beans, chickpeas, and lima beans as a standby for bulking out hearty soups in the winter months.

● Dried Herbs & Spices

A well-stocked pantry with dried spices should include smoked paprika, curry powder, cumin seeds, ground coriander, cumin, dried chiles or crushed red pepper flakes, and black peppercorns. Woody herbs, such as rosemary, thyme, and oregano, retain their flavor well in a dried format, but leafy herbs, such as cilantro, basil, and parsley, are best used fresh.

● Canned Ingredients

Canned tomatoes are an essential item on the weekly shop list, and these are available with extra flavorings, such as basil and garlic, which can save time. Jars or cans of sun-dried tomatoes in olive oil, roasted peppers, olives, capers, pesto, and anchovies are also useful to keep at home.

● Dried Pasta & Noodles

Dried soup pasta and most noodles are an ideal addition to soups (especially broths). You can also use regular dried pasta, but this takes longer to cook. Both pasta and noodles are handy because they have a long shelf life and a neutral flavor that goes well with stronger soups.

Using Leftovers

With rising food costs, trying to avoid food wastage has never been more important. Soup is the ideal vessel for freshening up old leftovers, and making the most out of what's sitting in the refrigerator.

Stale Bread

This is ideal for making bread crumbs—simply slice and place in a food processor or blender. Process until fine bread crumbs are created, then transfer to an airtight container and freeze for up to three months. Alternatively, use stale bread to make Crispy Pesto Croutons (page 292) or Italian-Style Bread Dumplings (page 288), which are delicious with soups and stews.

Cooked Meat

After a roasted dinner, don't throw away the scraps of meat: simply shred them, using two forks, transfer to an airtight container, and freeze for up to three months. This meat can be added to soup toward the end of cooking—serve when thoroughly reheated. The carcass of roasted poultry (such as chicken or turkey), beef bones, or fish bones are perfect for homemade stock—recipes are on pages 14 and 15.

Vegetables

Instead of using precooked vegetables for soup (which can lack flavor), it's better to use the scraps to boost the flavor of homemade stock. Keep the peels from carrots and potatoes to add to the Vegetable Stock recipe on page 15.

Cheese

Remember that Parmesan rind is a great source of flavor for soups, risottos, and sauces, so don't throw it away—add whole to soup along with the stock and remove before serving. Odd pieces of hard cheese can be shredded and stored in the freezer in an airtight container for up to six months. It can be used to top toasted bread to serve alongside soup, or on top of a dish—it's a good resource for when only a little strongly flavored cheese is needed.

Cooked Potatoes

You will find recipes in this book that use leftover cooked potatoes, such as the Potato Dumplings (page 286) and Potato Bread (page 278). Save yourself time in advance by prepping the cooked potatoes ready for use; mash while still warm, mix in a little butter and milk, and season

with salt and pepper. Then set the mashed potatoes aside and let cool completely. Once cooled, the mashed potatoes can be transferred to an airtight container and stored in the freezer for up to three months. Simply remove from the freezer and defrost overnight before use.

Cooked Pasta

It's not uncommon to find that you've cooked too much pasta, but this, too, can be stored as a useful time-saver. Simply drain any excess pasta thoroughly and set aside to cool completely. Once cold, it can be covered and kept in the refrigerator for up to three days. Alternatively, transfer to an airtight container and freeze for up to three months. Remove the container from the freezer and let the pasta defrost before use—add to the soup just before serving, stirring to mix through, and cook until the pasta is heated through.

Cooking Tips

Here are some hints and tips that might help to overcome some common problems that you may come across while making soup.

Thickening Soup

Nothing is more disappointing than finding that the soup you've worked so hard to perfect is a little on the thin side—but don't worry because there are some solutions to save your soup …

• Starch

Mix a little cornstarch with some cold water to form a smooth paste, then stir directly into the soup, stirring continuously, until the soup reaches the correct consistency. Alternatively, melt a little butter in a separate saucepan and stir in an equal amount of all-purpose flour—stir continuously over medium heat to make a smooth, thick paste. This can be whisked into the hot soup to thicken.

• Potato

Try grating a peeled raw potato into the soup, and cook for an additional 10–12 minutes, or until the potato is cooked through. If time is of the essence, add 1 tablespoon of dried mashed potato powder—stir continuously until evenly combined.

• Bread

For an almost instant thickening effect, add bread crumbs to the soup just before serving (ideally, made from slightly stale bread).

• Egg

You can use egg yolk to thicken soup—simply mix the raw yolk with 1 tablespoon of light cream in a large, heatproof bowl. Then add 1 tablespoon of the hot soup liquid to the egg mixture, whisking continuously until well mixed. Meanwhile, make sure that the soup is hot but not boiling, then add the egg mixture to the soup pan and stir to combine. Cook until the desired consistency is achieved, then serve.

• Pasta, Rice, & Beans

Adding starchy carbohydrates, such as uncooked pasta or rice, can help to thicken a soup—simply add to the pan before the end of the soup's cooking time the time specified on the package, and cook until the pasta or rice is tender but still firm to the bite. Or stir in drained canned beans in the last few minutes of cooking.

• Cream & Yogurt

Give a creamy finish to soup by adding heavy cream or Greek yogurt. Let the soup cool a little before adding these ingredients, and make sure the soup doesn't boil once combined.

If you're planning to make soup on a regular basis, invest in a food processor or handheld immersion blender; you can use these to shred and chop ingredients, as well as for processing soups to a smooth texture.

Rescuing Soup

Sometimes your soup needs a little TLC before it's ready to serve, but these troubleshooting tips should make sure you present perfect bowlfuls every time …

• Too Thick

Consider the ingredients in your soup before choosing what to add: for tomato-base soup, add water or vegetable stock; for creamier soups, add a little milk. Add any thinning agents a little at a time, stirring thoroughly after each addition—it is much easier to thin a soup than it is to thicken.

• Prevent Curdling

As a general rule, the lower the fat content of the cream or yogurt, the greater the chances that it will curdle. Once curdled, there's nothing you can do but start again (although it won't affect the taste of the soup). To avoid curdling, try an alternative to dairy—natural soy yogurt is a good enriching agent. Alternatively, be extra careful to cool the soup a little before adding the cream or yogurt, then reheat gently before serving, making sure that the mixture doesn't boil.

• Smooth Soup

In general, velvety smooth soups are created from using a food processor rather than a handheld immersion blender. However, after processing you may find that certain soups (particularly those made using "old" vegetables) remain a little stringy. To achieve a supersmooth texture, pass the soup through a fine-mesh strainer.

• Too Much Salt

Achieving the correct seasoning with salt and pepper is a matter of personal taste, so it is generally best to underseason soup before serving, because the dish can easily be seasoned at the table. It is difficult to remove a salty flavor from soup, but adding starchy carbohydrates, such as soup, potato, or rice, can help. Or try adding 1 teaspoon of white distilled vinegar to each quart of soup to balance the flavors.

Essential stock recipes

Beef stock

Makes about 5 cups

- 2 pounds beef bones, raw or cooked
- 1 large onion, coarsely chopped
- 1 large carrot, coarsely chopped
- 2 celery stalks, coarsely chopped
- 1 bouquet garni (made of 1 bay leaf, 3 black peppercorns, 2–3 fresh parsley sprigs, and 1 fresh thyme sprig tied in a cheesecloth bag)
- 7 cups water

1. Preheat the oven to 400°F. Put the bones in a roasting pan and cook in the preheated oven for 20 minutes, or until browned. Remove from the oven and let cool.

2. Chop the bones into small pieces and put in a large saucepan with the vegetables and bouquet garni. Pour in the water and bring to a boil, skimming off any foam that rises to the surface. Reduce the heat, cover, and simmer for 2 hours.

3. Strain the stock into a bowl and let cool. Cover and store in the refrigerator. When cold, remove and discard the layer of fat from the surface.

Chicken stock

Makes about 10 cups

- 1 (2¼-pound) chicken, cut into large pieces
- 17 cups water
- 3 carrots, coarsely chopped
- 5 shallots, coarsely chopped
- 1 onion, coarsely chopped
- 1 leek, coarsely chopped
- 2 celery stalks, coarsely chopped
- 1 garlic bulb
- 1 fresh rosemary sprig
- 1 fresh thyme sprig
- 2 bay leaves
- 1 teaspoon white peppercorns
- 5 cloves

1. Put the chicken into a large saucepan and pour in the water. Bring to a boil, skimming off any foam that rises to the surface.

2. Add the vegetables, garlic, rosemary, thyme, bay leaves, peppercorns, and cloves and simmer for 45 minutes.

3. Remove the chicken pieces and set aside for later use. Strain the stock into a bowl and let cool. Cover and store in the refrigerator. When cold, remove and discard the layer of fat from the surface.

Vegetable stock

Makes about 9 cups

- 10 cups water
- ½ fennel bulb, coarsely chopped
- 1 leek, coarsely chopped
- 3 carrots, coarsely chopped
- 2 celery stalks, coarsely chopped
- 2 onions, coarsely chopped
- 1 tomato, halved
- 1 garlic bulb, halved horizontally
- 1 fresh rosemary sprig
- 1 bay leaf
- 1 teaspoon white peppercorns
- ½ teaspoon fennel seeds

1. Pour the water into a large saucepan and add all the vegetables. Add the garlic, rosemary, bay leaf, peppercorns, and fennel seeds, bring to a boil, and simmer for 20 minutes.

2. Strain the stock into a bowl and let cool. Cover and store in the refrigerator.

Fish stock

Makes about 10 cups

- 2¼ pounds white fish heads, bones, and scraps, rinsed
- 3 tablespoons vegetable oil
- 1 onion, coarsely chopped
- 3 shallots, coarsely chopped
- ½ fennel bulb, coarsely chopped
- 3 celery stalks, coarsely chopped
- 1 garlic bulb, halved horizontally
- 10 white peppercorns
- ½ teaspoon fennel seeds
- 4 teaspoons sea salt
- 2 bay leaves
- 1 cup white wine
- ¼ cup dry vermouth
- 6 cups water
- 2 lemon slices
- 1 fresh basil sprig
- 1 fresh thyme sprig

1. Cut out and discard the gills from any fish heads, then soak the fish heads, bones, and scraps in cold water for 30 minutes.

2. Heat the oil in a large saucepan, add all the vegetables, and cook for 5 minutes, until softened but not browned. Add the garlic, peppercorns, fennel seeds, sea salt, and bay leaves.

3. Drain the fish well, then add to the pan and sweat briefly. Add the wine, vermouth, and water and slowly bring to a simmer, skimming off any foam that rises to the surface. Simmer gently for 15 minutes.

4. Add the lemon slices, basil, and thyme and simmer for an additional 5 minutes.

5. Strain the stock into a bowl and let cool. Cover and store in the refrigerator.

Once the homemade stock is completely cold, and any solidified fat has been skimmed from the surface, you can transfer the soup to an airtight container and keep in the freezer for up to six months. Simply remove from the freezer and let defrost completely overnight before use.

Spicy Chicken Noodle Soup 18

Rustic Bread, Basil & Tomato Soup 20

Ham & Lentil Soup 22

Cabbage & Smoky Bacon Soup 24

Mixed Squash Soup 26

Spiced Chickpea & Spinach Soup 28

Spicy Pepper & Tomato Soup 30

Fennel & Summer Vegetable Soup 32

Salmon & Udon Broth 34

Lemon, Chicken & Rice Soup 36

Chipotle, Chicken & Bean Soup 38

Orzo & Vegetable Soup 40

Squid, Chorizo & Tomato Soup 42

Lobster Bisque 44

Salmon Ramen Soup 46

Clam & Pasta Soup 48

Tomato & White Bean Soup 50

Leek & Potato Soup 52

Chunky Vegetable Soup 54

Fish Soup with Roasted Peppers & Harissa 56

Chorizo & Kale Soup 58

Scallop & Prosciutto Soup 60

Tomato Soup 62

Cream of Chicken Soup 64

Speedy Soups

Spicy Chicken Noodle Soup

 SERVES 2    PREP TIME: 15 minutes    COOKING TIME: 5–10 minutes

nutritional information **per serving** | 513 cal, 10.5g fat, 2.5g sat fat, 8.5g total sugars, 2.1g salt

This quick, healthy, wholesome soup is a real winner for an instant meal that's packed with goodness. The main flavor comes from miso, a highly nutritious fermented paste used as the basis of many noodle soups.

INGREDIENTS

1¼ cups chicken stock

1 tablespoon miso paste

¾-inch piece fresh ginger, peeled and finely grated

1 red chile, seeded and thinly sliced

1 carrot, peeled and cut into thin strips

3 cups coarsely chopped bok choy

6 ounces dried egg cellophane noodles, cooked

1 cooked chicken breast, shredded

dark soy sauce, to taste

4 scallions, trimmed and finely chopped

1. Pour the stock along with 1 cup of boiling water in a saucepan and bring to a boil over medium–high heat. Add the miso paste and simmer for 1–2 minutes.

2. Add the ginger, chile, carrot, bok choy, cooked noodles, and chicken. Simmer for an additional 4–5 minutes. Season with soy sauce.

3. Sprinkle the scallions over the bottom of two serving dishes and pour the soup over them. Serve immediately.

Rustic Bread, Basil & Tomato Soup

 SERVES 4  PREP TIME: 10 minutes  COOKING TIME: 25–30 minutes

nutritional information per serving	226 cal, 6g fat, 2g sat fat, 5.5g total sugars, 1.3g salt

Not only a great way of using up leftover bread, this soup is also a simple dinner to whip up if you're in a hurry—with very little prep needed.

INGREDIENTS

1 tablespoon olive oil

1 onion, finely chopped

2 cloves garlic, crushed

1 (14½-ounce) can whole plum tomatoes

2½ cups chicken stock or vegetable stock

7 slices day-old, unsliced white bread, cubed

handful fresh basil, coarsely chopped, plus extra to garnish

salt and pepper, to taste

Parmesan cheese, to serve

1. Heat the oil in a saucepan over medium heat. Add the onion and garlic and sauté for 4–5 minutes.

2. Add the tomatoes and stock, and use the back of a wooden spoon to break the tomatoes apart. Season with salt and pepper, cover, and simmer for 15 minutes.

3. Add the bread and basil and simmer for an additional 5 minutes.

4. Serve with Parmesan cheese shavings sprinkled over the top, garnished with the chopped basil and seasoned with pepper.

1

2

3

SOMETHING DIFFERENT

If you have a bumper crop of fresh tomatoes to use up, toss four of them in a little oil, then roast in a hot oven for about 20 minutes. Add to the soup in place of the canned tomatoes.

Ham & Lentil Soup

 SERVES 2   PREP TIME: 10 minutes   COOKING TIME: 25–30 minutes

nutritional information per serving	374 cal, 11.5g fat, 2.5g sat fat, 5.5g total sugars, 3.5g salt

Transform cold, cooked meats into a healthy, hearty winter meal packed with goodness that will leave you feeling full and contented.

INGREDIENTS

8 ounces cooked ham

1 tablespoon vegetable oil

1 onion, finely chopped

1 clove garlic, finely chopped

1 carrot, finely diced

1 celery stalk, thinly sliced

1 (15-ounce) can green lentils, drained

1 teaspoon finely chopped fresh rosemary leaves,

2½ cups vegetable stock or ham stock

pepper, to taste

1. Using two forks, finely shred the cooked ham and set aside.

2. Heat the oil in a saucepan over medium–high heat. Add the onion, garlic, carrot, and celery and sauté for 4–5 minutes, or until starting to soften.

3. Add the lentils, rosemary, shredded ham, and stock, and season with pepper. Cover and simmer for 20 minutes, or until the vegetables are just tender. Serve immediately.

1

2

3

FREEZING TIP
Freeze for up to
six months in an
airtight container.
Defrost completely
and reheat to serve.

Cabbage & Smoky Bacon Soup

 SERVES 4　　 PREP TIME: 15 minutes　　 COOKING TIME: 25–30 minutes

nutritional information per serving	330 cal, 18.5g fat, 6g sat fat, 8.5g total sugars, 2.9g salt

A flavorsome soup that packs a punch—perfect served with warm tear-and-share bread or some crispy croutons.

INGREDIENTS

1 tablespoon vegetable oil

2 cloves garlic, crushed

1 onion, peeled and finely chopped

2 celery stalks, chopped

8 ounces smoked bacon, chopped

1 savoy cabbage, cored and shredded

5½ cups chicken stock

1 teaspoon Worcestershire sauce

pepper, to taste

2 tablespoons chopped fresh flat-leaf parsley, to serve

1. Heat the oil in a large skillet over medium–high heat. Add the garlic, onion, and celery and sauté for 4–5 minutes, or until softened.

2. Add the bacon and sauté for an additional 3–4 minutes, or until starting to brown.

3. Add the cabbage, stock, and Worcestershire sauce and season with pepper. Cover and simmer for 15–20 minutes.

4. Process in a blender or food processor until smooth. Serve with the parsley sprinkled over the soup.

2

3

4

Mixed Squash Soup

 SERVES 4    PREP TIME: 20 minutes    COOKING TIME: 25–30 minutes

nutritional information per serving	169 cal, 7g fat, 2.5g sat fat, 14.5g total sugars, 0.7g salt

Squash makes superb soups with a velvety texture and vivid colors. Mixing the different types gives more interest and flavor, so try buying a selection of what is in season.

INGREDIENTS

1 tablespoon vegetable oil

1 large onion, chopped

1 celery stalk, chopped

2 carrots, chopped

2 cloves garlic, crushed

6 cups peeled, seeded, and cubed mixed winter squash, such as butternut, acorn, delicata, or kabocha squash

4 cups vegetable stock

1 tablespoon fresh thyme leaves, finely chopped

salt and pepper, to taste

crème fraiche or Greek yogurt, to serve

1. Heat the oil in a large saucepan over medium–high heat. Add the onion, celery, and carrots and sweat for 3–4 minutes, or until starting to soften.

2. Add the garlic and squash, and sauté for an additional minute. Add the stock and thyme and season with salt and pepper. Bring to a boil, cover, and simmer for 20 minutes, or until the vegetables are tender.

3. Process using a handheld immersion blender until smooth. Serve immediately, topped with dollop of crème fraiche or Greek yogurt.

1

2

3

GOES WELL WITH

Serve in the hollowed out crust of a crusty round loaf. Remove the soft inside of the bread with a spoon and set aside to make croutons to serve with the soup.

Spiced Chickpea & Spinach Soup

 SERVES 4   PREP TIME: 5 minutes   COOKING TIME: 20–25 minutes

nutritional information per serving	181 cal, 6.5g fat, 1g sat fat, 6.5g total sugars, 1g salt

Enjoy a warming blend of aromatic herbs and spices. The addition of the mint dressing makes a delicious, cooling topping that complements the subtle heat of the soup.

INGREDIENTS

1 tablespoon vegetable oil

1 onion, finely chopped

2 cloves garlic, crushed

1 teaspoon whole cumin seeds

2 teaspoons medium curry powder

1 teaspoon hot chili powder

1 (15-ounce) can chickpeas, rinsed and drained

1 (14½-ounce) can diced tomatoes

2 cups vegetable stock

3½ cups chopped spinach, thawed if frozen

salt and pepper, to taste

mint dressing
½ cup plain yogurt

2 tablespoons fresh mint leaves, finely chopped

1. Heat the oil in a saucepan over medium heat. Add the onion and sauté for 4–5 minutes, or until starting to soften.

2. Add the garlic, cumin seeds, curry powder, and chili powder and cook for 1 minute, stirring continuously.

3. Add the chickpeas, tomatoes, and stock and season with salt and pepper. Bring to a boil, then reduce the heat, cover, and simmer for 15 minutes.

4. Meanwhile, to make the mint dressing, add the yogurt and mint to a bowl, season with salt and pepper, and mix together. Cover and chill until ready to serve.

5. Stir the spinach into the soup and cook for an additional 1–2 minutes, or until the spinach has wilted. Serve with a little of the mint dressing drizzled over the soup.

Spicy Pepper & Tomato Soup

 SERVES 4    PREP TIME: 5 minutes   COOKING TIME: 20–25 minutes

nutritional information per serving	125 cal, 4g fat, 0.5g sat fat, 13.5g total sugars, 0.5g salt

This vibrant soup is packed with health-boosting antioxidants, plus it's incredibly quick to make because it uses store-bought roasted red peppers; a great pantry standby for speedy dinners.

INGREDIENTS

1 tablespoon vegetable oil

1 onion, chopped

2 cloves garlic, chopped

1½ teaspoons hot chili powder

2 tablespoons tomato paste

2¼ cups drained and chopped roasted red peppers

1 (28-ounce) can diced tomatoes

1¾ cups vegetable stock

salt and pepper, to taste

1. Heat the oil in a saucepan over medium heat. Add the onion and garlic and sauté for 3–4 minutes, until starting to soften.

2. Add the chili powder and tomato paste and cook for 1 minute, stirring continuously.

3. Add the roasted red peppers, tomatoes, and stock and season with salt and pepper. Stir well, cover, and simmer for 15 minutes.

4. Process in a blender or food processor, until smooth. Adjust the seasoning, if necessary, and serve.

1

2

3

GOES WELL WITH

Delicious served with goat cheese crumbled over the top, and a generous drizzle of olive oil.

Fennel & Summer Vegetable Soup

 SERVES 4  PREP TIME: 20 minutes  COOKING TIME: 20–25 minutes

nutritional information per serving | 207 cal, 4g fat, 0.7g sat fat, 4.5g total sugars, 0.8g salt

Wonderfully fresh and light, and bursting with the flavors of summer, this soup is delicious to eat and sturdy enough to fill you until dinner.

INGREDIENTS

1 tablespoon vegetable oil
1 onion, finely chopped
2 cloves garlic, crushed
1 whole fennel bulb, trimmed and diced
1 leek, finely sliced
1 large potato, diced
4 cups vegetable stock
3½ cups spinach, trimmed
6 asparagus spears, trimmed and cut into short lengths
1⅓ cups frozen peas
handful fresh basil leaves, thinly sliced
salt and pepper, to taste

1. Heat the oil in a saucepan over medium heat and sauté the onion for 5 minutes. Add the garlic, fennel, leek, and potato and cook for an additional 1–2 minutes.

2. Add the stock and season with salt and pepper. Cover and simmer for 15 minutes.

3. Add the spinach, asparagus, and peas and cook for an additional 2–3 minutes.

4. Stir in the basil leaves, adjust the seasoning, if necessary, and serve.

Salmon & Udon Broth

 SERVES 4    PREP TIME: 10 minutes    COOKING TIME: 15–20 minutes

nutritional information per serving	431 cal, 8g fat, 1.5g sat fat, 7g total sugars, 2.9g salt

Udon noodles are made from wheat and tend to be thicker and more substantial than regular noodles. They work well in this recipe, making a complete meal in a bowl, which is low in fat but high in nutrients.

INGREDIENTS

4 cups vegetable stock

1-inch piece fresh ginger, thinly sliced

6 scallions, finely chopped

2 carrots, cut into thin sticks

2 tablespoons miso paste

8 ounces dried udon noodles

9 ounces fresh salmon fillet, cubed

4 ounces shitake mushrooms, sliced

1 fresh red chile, seeded and thinly sliced, to garnish

dark soy sauce, to taste

1. Put the stock in a saucepan with the ginger, scallions, carrots, and miso paste and bring to a boil over medium–high heat.

2. Meanwhile, cook the noodles in a separate saucepan of boiling water according to the package directions until tender. Drain, return to the pan, and keep covered until ready to serve.

3. Add the salmon and mushrooms to the broth and cook for 2–3 minutes, until the salmon is cooked through and flakes easily.

4. Divide the cooked noodles among four bowls and top with the salmon broth. Garnish with a little chile and season with soy sauce.

Lemon, Chicken & Rice Soup

SERVES 4   PREP TIME: 10 minutes   COOKING TIME: 15–20 minutes

nutritional information per serving	341 cal, 6.5g fat, 1.5g sat fat, 3g total sugars, 0.9g salt

This soup is packed with fresh flavors—lifted by a zingy dose of lemon juice.

INGREDIENTS

1 tablespoon vegetable oil

1 onion, finely chopped

1 leek, finely chopped

1 clove garlic, crushed

finely grated zest and juice of ½ lemon

½ cup long-grain rice

4 cups chicken stock

2 cooked chicken breasts, coarsely chopped

3½ cups fresh spinach

1 cup frozen peas

¼ cup chopped fresh flat-leaf parsley

salt and pepper, to taste

Parmesan cheese, to serve

1. Heat the oil in a large saucepan over medium heat. Sauté the onion and leek for 4–5 minutes, until starting to soften. Add the garlic and lemon zest and cook for an additional 1–2 minutes.

2. Add the rice and stock and bring to a boil. Cover and simmer for 8 minutes. Add the chicken, spinach, and peas and season with salt and pepper. Cook for an additional 4 minutes, until the rice is cooked through.

3. Stir in the lemon juice and parsley and serve with some Parmesan cheese shavings sprinkled on top.

COOK'S NOTE
Only add the lemon juice when you are just about to serve the soup, otherwise it will cause the green vegetables to lose their color.

Chipotle, Chicken & Bean Soup

 SERVES 4

 PREP TIME:
5 minutes

 COOKING TIME:
20–25 minutes

nutritional information per serving	230 cal, 5.5g fat, 1g sat fat, 12g total sugars, 1.3g salt

A hearty, yet simple dinner with virtually no preparation, the smoky chipotle heat sits well with the tomatoes and beans to make a rich thick meal in a bowl.

INGREDIENTS

1 tablespoon vegetable oil

1 small onion, finely chopped

2 cloves garlic, crushed

1 teaspoon whole cumin seeds

1 tablespoon chipotle paste, or to taste

1 tablespoon tomato paste

½ cup drained and sliced roasted red peppers

1 (14½-ounce) can diced tomatoes

1 cup drained, canned corn kernels

1 (15-ounce) can kidney beans, rinsed and drained

1 cup cooked chicken strips

fresh flat-leaf parsley, finely chopped, to serve

salt and pepper, to taste

1. Heat the oil in a saucepan over medium heat and sauté the onion for 3–4 minutes, until starting to soften.

2. Add the garlic and cumin seeds and cook for an additional minute, then add the chipotle and tomato paste and cook for 1 minute, stirring all the time.

3. Add the roasted red pepper and tomatoes, and season with salt and pepper. Cover and simmer for 10–15 minutes.

4. Stir in the corn, kidney beans, and chicken and reduce the heat to medium–low. Cook for an additional 4–5 minutes. Sprinkle with parsley to serve.

Orzo & Vegetable Soup

 SERVES 2 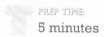 PREP TIME: 5 minutes  COOKING TIME: 15–20 minutes

nutritional information per serving	382 cal, 7g fat, 1g sat fat, 11g total sugars, 1.3g salt

Orzo is a tiny pasta, shaped like little grains of rice. It's quick to cook and perfect to help add texture and bulk to a variety of soups and stews.

INGREDIENTS

1 tablespoon olive oil

1 bunch scallions, finely chopped

3½ cups vegetable stock

4 ounces dried orzo

1 cup drained and sliced roasted red peppers

1 cup trimmed green bean pieces

3 cups coarsely chopped spinach, thawed if frozen

salt and pepper, to taste

Parmesan cheese, to serve

extra virgin olive oil, to serve

1. Heat the oil in a saucepan over medium–high heat, add the scallions, and sauté for 2–3 minutes, or until starting to soften.

2. Add the stock and orzo and bring to a boil. Season with salt and pepper, then cover and simmer for 8 minutes.

3. Add the roasted peppers, beans, and spinach and cook for an additional 2–3 minutes, then taste and adjust the seasoning, if necessary. Serve with Parmesan cheese shavings and a drizzle of olive oil.

GOES WELL WITH
Serve with warm focaccia bread, topped with grated Parmesan cheese and broiled for 1-2 minutes, or until the cheese has melted.

Squid, Chorizo & Tomato Soup

 SERVES 6    PREP TIME: 20 minutes   COOKING TIME: 40–45 minutes

nutritional information
per serving   200 cal, 7g fat, 3g sat fat, 4.5g total sugars, 1.2g salt

A rich aromatic tomato soup in which the spicy, salty chorizo provides a wonderful contrast to the tender squid, making a delicious speedy treat.

INGREDIENTS

1 pound cleaned squid

6 ounces lean chorizo, peeled and finely diced

1 onion, finely chopped

1 celery stalk, thinly sliced

1 carrot, thinly sliced

2 cloves garlic, finely chopped

1 (14½-ounce) can diced tomatoes

5 cups fish stock

½ teaspoon ground cumin

pinch of saffron

1 bay leaf

hot pepper sauce, to taste

salt and pepper, to taste

fresh chopped flat-leaf parsley, to garnish

1. Cut off the squid tentacles and cut into bite-size pieces. Slice the bodies into rings.

2. Put a large saucepan over medium–low heat and add the chorizo. Cook for 5–10 minutes, stirring frequently, until it renders most of its fat. Remove with a slotted spoon and drain on paper towels.

3. Pour off all the fat from the pan and add the onion, celery, carrot, and garlic. Cover and cook for 3–4 minutes, until the onion is slightly softened.

4. Stir in the tomatoes, fish stock, cumin, saffron, bay leaf, and chorizo.

5. Add the squid to the soup. Bring almost to a boil, reduce the heat, cover, and cook gently for 30–35 minutes, or until the squid and carrot are tender, stirring occasionally. Remove and discard the bay leaf.

6. Stir in hot pepper sauce for a spicier flavor and season with salt and pepper. Ladle into warm bowls, sprinkle with parsley, and serve immediately.

Lobster Bisque

 SERVES 4

 PREP TIME:
20 minutes

 COOKING TIME:
45–50 minutes

nutritional information per serving	454 cal, 24g fat, 14g sat fat, 5g total sugars, 1.1g salt

This elegant, smooth, and delicious soup is perfect for entertaining and bound to impress your guests.

INGREDIENTS

1 pound cooked lobster
3 tablespoons butter
1 small carrot, shredded
1 celery stalk, finely chopped
1 leek, finely chopped
1 small onion, finely chopped
2 shallots, finely chopped
3 tablespoons brandy or Cognac
¼ cup dry white wine
5 cups water
1 tablespoon tomato paste
½ cup heavy cream, or to taste
⅓ cup all-purpose flour
2–3 tablespoons water
salt and pepper, to taste
snipped fresh chives, to garnish

1. Pull off the lobster tail. With the legs up, cut the body in half lengthwise. Scoop out the tomalley and the roe. Reserve these, cover, and chill in the refrigerator. Remove the meat from the rest of the lobster and cut into bite-size pieces, then cover and chill in the refrigerator. Chop the shell into large pieces.

2. Melt half the butter in a large saucepan over medium heat and add the lobster shell pieces. Sauté until brown pieces begin to stick to the bottom of the pan. Add the carrot, celery, leek, onion, and shallots. Cook, stirring continuously, for 1–2 minutes. Add the brandy and wine and simmer for 1 minute. Pour in the water, add the tomato paste and a large pinch of salt, and bring to a boil. Reduce the heat and simmer for 30 minutes, then strain the stock, discarding the solids.

3. Melt the remaining butter in a small saucepan and add the tomalley and roe. Add the cream and whisk to mix well, then remove from the heat and set aside. Put the flour in a small mixing bowl and slowly whisk in the cold water. Stir in a little of the hot stock mixture to make a smooth liquid.

4. Bring the remaining lobster stock to a boil and whisk in the flour mixture. Boil gently for 4–5 minutes, or until the soup thickens. Press the tomalley, roe, and cream mixture through a strainer into the soup, then add the lobster meat. Simmer until heated through.

5. Taste and adjust the seasoning, adding salt and pepper, if needed. Stir in a little more cream, if desired. Ladle into warm bowls, garnish with chives, and serve immediately.

Salmon Ramen Soup

 SERVES 4    PREP TIME: 10 minutes    COOKING TIME: 20–25 minutes

nutritional information per serving	500 cal, 19g fat, 3.5g sat fat, 5g total sugars, 2.9g salt

In this recipe, the salmon is broiled in a sweet sticky teriyaki marinade and served on a bowl of broth with egg noodles and Asian spices. It's warming, satisfying, and easy to prepare.

INGREDIENTS

4 cups vegetable stock

1 clove garlic

½ teaspoon light soy sauce

4 salmon fillets, about 5 ounces each, skinned

sunflower oil, for brushing

5 ounces dried ramen noodles

3½ cups baby spinach leaves

4 scallions, finely chopped

teriyaki glaze

2½ tablespoons sake

2½ tablespoons dark soy sauce

2 tablespoons mirin or sweet sherry

1½ teaspoons packed light brown sugar

½ clove garlic, minced

¼-inch piece fresh ginger, minced

to serve

1 cup fresh bean sprouts

1 fresh green chile, seeded and sliced

fresh cilantro leaves

1. Preheat the broiler to high. Put the stock in a saucepan, add the garlic clove and soy sauce, and bring to a boil. Remove from the heat and set aside.

2. Mix together the ingredients for the teriyaki glaze and brush one surface of each salmon fillet with the glaze. Lightly brush the broiler rack with oil and cook the salmon under the preheated broiler for 4 minutes on only one side. The fish should be almost cooked through and flake easily. Remove from the broiler and set aside.

3. Meanwhile, cook the noodles in a saucepan of boiling water according to the package directions, until tender.

4. Remove the garlic from the stock, then bring the stock back to a boil. Drop in the spinach leaves and scallions and cook until the leaves are just wilted. Use a slotted spoon to remove the spinach and scallions from the pan and divide them among warm bowls. Divide the noodles among the bowls, then add a salmon fillet to each. Carefully pour the boiling stock into each bowl.

5. Sprinkle with the bean sprouts, chile, and cilantro leaves and serve immediately.

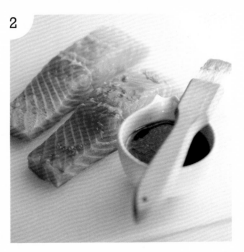

Clam & Pasta Soup

 SERVES 6

 PREP TIME:
10 minutes

 COOKING TIME:
30–35 minutes

nutritional information per serving	212 cal, 6.5g fat, 1g sat fat, 6.5g total sugars, 0.8g salt

A great way to feed a hungry crowd using fresh clams when in season. Make sure you have some warm crusty bread standing by to mop up all the delicious flavors.

INGREDIENTS

3 tablespoons olive oil

1 Spanish onion, finely chopped

3 cloves garlic, finely chopped

2½ cups canned diced tomatoes

2 tablespoons tomato paste

2 teaspoons sugar

1 teaspoon dried oregano

4 cups vegetable stock

1 pound fresh clams, scrubbed

¾ cup dry white wine

3 ounces dried conchigliette

3 tablespoons chopped fresh flat-leaf parsley

salt and pepper, to taste

1. Heat the oil in a large saucepan. Add the onion and garlic and cook over low heat, stirring occasionally, for 5 minutes, until softened. Add the tomatoes, tomato paste, sugar, oregano, and stock and season with salt and pepper. Mix well and bring to a boil, then reduce the heat, cover, and simmer, stirring occasionally, for 5 minutes.

2. Discard any clams with broken shells and any that refuse to close when tapped. Put the clams into a saucepan, pour in the wine, cover, and cook over high heat, shaking the pan occasionally, for 3–5 minutes.

3. Remove the clams from the heat and remove from the liquid with a slotted spoon. Reserve the cooking liquid. Discard any clams that remain closed and remove the remainder from the half shells. Strain the reserved cooking liquid through a cheesecloth-lined strainer into a bowl and set aside.

4. Add the pasta to the soup and simmer, uncovered, for 10 minutes. Add the cooked clams and the reserved cooking liquid. Stir well and heat gently for 4–5 minutes; do not let the soup come back to a boil. Taste and adjust the seasoning, if necessary, stir in the parsley, and serve immediately.

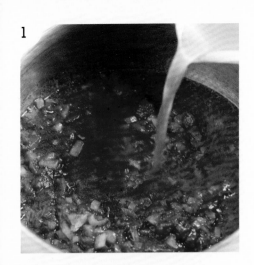

Tomato & White Bean Soup

 SERVES 6

 PREP TIME:
30 minutes

 COOKING TIME:
30–35 minutes

nutritional information **per serving**	240 cal, 9g fat, 2.5g sat fat, 12g total sugars, 0.7g salt

This recipe is perfect for using up a bumper crop of tomatoes in the late summer and is also low in fat.

INGREDIENTS

3 tablespoons olive oil

2 red onions, finely chopped

1 celery stalk, finely chopped

1 red bell pepper, seeded and finely chopped

2 cloves garlic, finely chopped

16 plum tomatoes, peeled and chopped

5½ cups vegetable stock

2 tablespoons tomato paste

1 teaspoon sugar

1 tablespoon sweet paprika

1 tablespoon butter

1 tablespoon all-purpose flour

1 (15-ounce) can cannellini beans, rinsed and drained

salt and pepper, to taste

chopped fresh flat-leaf parsley, to garnish

1. Heat the olive oil in a large saucepan. Add the onions, celery, red bell pepper, and garlic and cook over low heat, stirring occasionally, for 5 minutes, until softened.

2. Increase the heat to medium, add the tomatoes, and cook, stirring occasionally, for an additional 5 minutes, then pour in the stock. Stir in the tomato paste, sugar, and sweet paprika and season with salt and pepper. Bring to a boil, reduce the heat, and simmer for 15 minutes.

3. Meanwhile, mash together the butter and flour to a paste in a small bowl with a fork. Stir the paste, small pieces at a time, into the soup. Make sure each piece is fully incorporated before adding the next.

4. Add the beans, stir well, and simmer for an additional 5 minutes, until heated through. Sprinkle with the parsley and serve immediately.

Leek & Potato Soup

 SERVES 6　　 PREP TIME: 15 minutes　　 COOKING TIME: 20–25 minutes

nutritional information per serving	195 cal, 13g fat, 8g sat fat, 3g total sugars, 0.6g salt

This soup has a velvety texture and mild flavor that makes it wonderful for warming you up in the depths of winter—which is especially good, because this is when leeks are at their best flavor and price.

INGREDIENTS

4 tablespoons butter

1 onion, chopped

3 leeks, sliced

2 Yukon gold, red-skinned, or white round potatoes, cut into ¾-inch cubes

3½ cups vegetable stock

salt and pepper, to taste

⅔ cup light cream, to serve

snipped fresh chives, to garnish

1. Melt the butter in a large saucepan over medium heat, add the onion, leeks, and potatoes, and sauté gently for 2–3 minutes, until soft but not brown. Pour in the stock, bring to a boil, then reduce the heat and simmer, covered, for 15 minutes.

2. Process using a handheld immersion blender, until smooth.

3. Heat the soup gently and season with salt and pepper. Ladle into warm bowls, garnish with a swirl of cream and snipped chives, and serve immediately.

FREEZING TIP
This soup is great to have as a freezer standby. Chill after cooking and pour into an airtight container or a large pitcher lined with a plastic food bag. Seal and freeze for up to three months.

Chunky Vegetable Soup

 SERVES 4

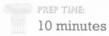 PREP TIME: 10 minutes

 COOKING TIME: 15–20 minutes

nutritional information per serving	113 cal, 6g fat, 0.7g sat fat, 8g total sugars, 0.4g salt

This is a hearty, satisfying soup that makes a colorful and nutritious lunch any day of the week. Add seasonal vegetables to make a meal fit for any weather.

INGREDIENTS

1 red onion
1 celery stalk
1 zucchini
2 carrots
2 tablespoons sunflower oil
1 (14½-ounce) can diced tomatoes
3¼ cups vegetable stock
1 large sprig of fresh thyme
salt and pepper, to taste
chopped fresh thyme, to garnish

1. Cut the onion, celery, zucchini, and carrots into ½-inch cubes.

2. Heat the oil in a large saucepan over medium heat. Add the vegetables and sauté, stirring, for 5 minutes without browning.

3. Add the tomatoes, stock, and the thyme sprig. Bring to a boil, then reduce the heat. Cover and simmer for 10–15 minutes, until the vegetables are just tender. Remove and discard the thyme sprig and season with salt and pepper.

4. Transfer the soup to warm serving bowls. Garnish with chopped thyme and serve immediately.

1

2

3

COOK'S NOTE
If fresh thyme is not available, use 1 teaspoon of dried thyme instead. A sprinkling of freshly chopped parsley is good for a fresh garnish.

Fish Soup with Roasted Peppers & Harissa

 SERVES 6

PREP TIME:
20 minutes

COOKING TIME:
20–25 minutes

nutritional information **per serving** | 375 cal, 8g fat, 1g sat fat, 9g total sugars, 1.1g salt

Choose your favorite firm white fish and shellfish in this mildly spiced yet full-flavored soup. Charring the bell peppers adds a depth of flavor and brings out their sweetness.

INGREDIENTS

2 red or yellow bell peppers

2¼ pounds firm white fish, such as cod, halibut, red snapper, and sea bass, and shellfish, such as shrimp, mussels, and clams

3 tablespoons olive oil

1 onion, finely chopped

3 cloves garlic, finely chopped

2 teaspoons harissa

1 small bunch of fresh flat-leaf parsley, finely chopped

3½ cups fish stock

¾ cup white wine (optional)

1 (14½-ounce) can diced tomatoes, drained

salt and pepper, to taste

fresh cilantro, coarsely chopped, to garnish

1. Using tongs, carefully hold the bell peppers directly over a gas flame, or cook under a preheated high broiler or on a barbecue, turning frequently, for 6–8 minutes, or until the skin blisters and turns black. Put the charred bell peppers in a plastic bag and let sweat for 5 minutes, then hold by the stems under cold running water and peel off the skins. Put the bell peppers on a cutting board, remove the stems and seeds, and cut the flesh into thick strips. Set aside.

2. Cut the fish into large chunks and clean and prepare any shellfish. Discard any mussels and clams with broken shells and any that refuse to close when tapped. Cover and chill until required.

3. Heat the oil in a deep, heavy casserole dish or saucepan, add the onion and garlic, and cook over medium heat, stirring frequently, for 2–3 minutes, until they begin to brown. Add the harissa and parsley, and pour in the stock.

4. Bring to a boil, then reduce the heat and simmer for 10 minutes, until the flavors are absorbed.

5. Add the wine, if using, and the tomatoes. Gently stir in the fish, shellfish, and the charred peppers and bring back to a boil. Reduce the heat, season with salt and pepper, and simmer for about 5 minutes, until the fish is cooked through. Discard any mussels and clams that remain closed. Ladle into warm bowls, garnish with the cilantro, and serve immediately.

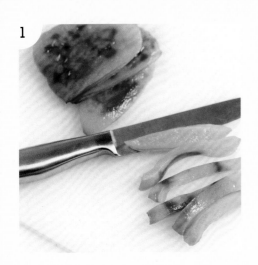

Chorizo & Kale Soup

SERVES 6 | PREP TIME: 20 minutes | COOKING TIME: 25–30 minutes

nutritional information per serving	317 cal, 14g fat, 3g sat fat, 2.5g total sugars, 1g salt

This vibrant, colorful soup combines nutrient-packed greens with crispy spiced chorizo.

INGREDIENTS

3 tablespoons olive oil, plus extra for drizzling

1 Spanish onion, finely chopped

2 cloves garlic, finely chopped

8 Yukon gold, red-skinned, or white round potatoes (about 2 pounds), diced

6 cups vegetable stock

4 ounces chorizo, thinly sliced

7 cups shredded kale (about 1 pound)

salt and pepper, to taste

1. Heat 2 tablespoons of the oil in a large saucepan. Add the onion and garlic and cook over low heat, stirring occasionally, for 5 minutes, until softened. Add the potatoes and cook for an additional 3 minutes.

2. Increase the heat to medium, pour in the stock, and bring to a boil. Reduce the heat, cover, and cook for 10 minutes.

3. Meanwhile, heat the remaining oil in a skillet. Add the chorizo and cook over low heat, turning occasionally, for a few minutes, until the fat runs. Remove with a slotted spoon and drain on paper towels.

4. Remove the pan of soup from the heat and mash the potatoes with a potato masher. Return to the heat, add the kale, and bring back to a boil. Reduce the heat and simmer for 5–6 minutes, until tender.

5. Remove the pan from the heat and mash the potatoes again. Stir in the chorizo, season with salt and pepper, and ladle into warm bowls. Drizzle with a little oil and serve immediately.

1

3

5

COOK'S NOTE
Chorizo is available in a variety of forms; this recipe uses the precooked sausage. A brief sauté in a hot pan releases its oil and produces a crisp texture.

Scallop & Prosciutto Soup

nutritional information per serving	445 cal, 15g fat, 8.5g sat fat, 4.5g total sugars, 1.6g salt

Sweet scallops combine with the salty Italian prosciutto and fine pasta to make a quick yet substantial soup.

INGREDIENTS

1 pound shucked scallops

1½ cups milk

6 cups fish stock

1⅔ cups frozen green peas

6 ounces dried tagliolini

5 tablespoons butter

2 scallions, finely chopped

¾ cup dry white wine

3 slices of prosciutto, chopped

salt and pepper, to taste

chopped fresh flat-leaf parsley, to garnish

1. Slice the scallops in half horizontally and season with salt and pepper.

2. Pour the milk and stock into a saucepan, add a pinch of salt, and bring to a boil. Add the peas and pasta, bring back to a boil, and cook according to the package directions, until the pasta is tender but still firm to the bite.

3. Meanwhile, melt the butter in a skillet. Add the scallions and cook over low heat, stirring occasionally, for 3 minutes. Add the scallops and cook for 45 seconds on each side. Pour in the wine, add the prosciutto, and cook for an additional 2–3 minutes.

4. Stir the scallop mixture into the soup. Taste and adjust the seasoning, adding salt and pepper, if needed. Ladle into warm bowls, garnish with parsley, and serve immediately.

2

3

4

COOK'S NOTE
This recipe calls for just the white part of the scallop, not the coral, which is ideal for using frozen scallops— plus they're much easier to store before use.

Tomato Soup

 SERVES 4

 PREP TIME:
5 minutes

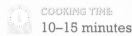 COOKING TIME:
10–15 minutes

nutritional information
per serving   100 cal, 6g fat, 0.8g sat fat, 5.5g total sugars, 0.4g salt

This soup is ready in minutes and made with pantry ingredients, perfect for a warming lunch or a quick appetizer.

INGREDIENTS

2 tablespoons olive oil
1 large onion, chopped
1 (14½-ounce) can whole plum tomatoes
1¼ cups vegetable stock
1 tablespoon tomato paste
1 teaspoon hot pepper sauce
handful of fresh basil leaves
salt and pepper, to taste

1. Heat the oil in a large saucepan over medium heat, then add the onion and sauté for 4–5 minutes, stirring, until soft. Add the tomatoes, stock, tomato paste, hot pepper sauce, and half the basil leaves.

2. Process using a handheld immersion blender until smooth. Stir the soup over medium heat until just boiling, then season with salt and pepper.

3. Serve the soup in warm serving bowls, garnished with the remaining basil leaves.

GOES WELL WITH Toasted whole-wheat bread with shredded cheddar cheese.

Cream of Chicken Soup

 SERVES 4   PREP TIME: 15 minutes    COOKING TIME: 40–45 minutes

nutritional information per serving	463 cal, 34g fat, 21g sat fat, 2g total sugars, 0.8g salt

Chicken soup is the ultimate comfort food for winter days, and you can whip this up in under an hour.

INGREDIENTS

3 tablespoons butter

4 shallots, chopped

1 leek, sliced

1 pound skinless, boneless chicken breasts, chopped

2½ cups chicken stock

1 tablespoon chopped fresh parsley

1 tablespoon chopped fresh thyme, plus extra sprigs to garnish

¼ cup heavy cream

salt and pepper, to taste

1. Melt the butter in a large saucepan over medium heat. Add the shallots and cook, stirring, for 3 minutes, until slightly softened. Then add the leek and cook for an additional 5 minutes, stirring occasionally.

2. Add the chicken, stock, and herbs, and season with salt and pepper. Bring to a boil, then reduce the heat and simmer for 25 minutes, until the chicken is tender and cooked through.

3. Remove from the heat and let cool for 10 minutes. Transfer to a food processor or blender, in batches if necessary, and process until smooth. Return the soup to the rinsed-out pan and warm over low heat for 5 minutes.

4. Stir in the cream and cook for an additional 2 minutes, then remove from the heat and ladle into serving bowls. Garnish with thyme sprigs and serve immediately.

1

2

4

Roasted Tomato & Pesto Soup *68*

Chilled Avocado Soup *70*

Edamame Soup with Spinach & Basil *72*

Chile Chicken Soup *74*

Ham & Black-Eyed Pea Soup *76*

Lettuce & Arugula Soup *78*

Curried Zucchini Soup *80*

Southwest Vegetable Soup *82*

Avocado Soup with Guacamole Toasts *84*

Salmon & Leek Soup *86*

Chilled Fava Bean Soup *88*

Asparagus Soup *90*

Crab & Ginger Soup *92*

Summer Vegetable Soup with Pistou Sauce *94*

Potato & Pesto Soup *96*

Pea Soup *98*

Chilled Red Pepper Soup *100*

Hot & Sour Soup with Salmon *102*

Chicken, Avocado & Chipotle Soup *104*

Chicken & Lemon Soup *106*

Chicken & Collard Greens Soup *108*

White Bean Soup *110*

Chilled Pea Soup *112*

Chilled Melon Soup *114*

Summer Soups

Roasted Tomato & Pesto Soup

 SERVES 4

 PREP TIME:
10 minutes

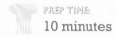 COOKING TIME:
25–30 minutes

nutritional information
per serving · 184 cal, 10.4g fat, 0.6g sat fat, 9g total sugars, 0.6g salt

This soup provides a real taste of summer, and it is a great way to use up a bumper crop of tomatoes from the garden. It's also a light, healthy option, packed with antioxidants, vitamins, and minerals.

INGREDIENTS

1 tablespoon extra virgin olive oil
2 red onions, cut into small wedges
2 cloves garlic, crushed
6 ripe tomatoes
2 cups vegetable stock
salt and pepper, to taste
pesto, to garnish

1. Preheat the oven to 400°F.

2. Put the oil, onions, garlic, and tomatoes in a small roasting pan and toss well to coat. Season generously with salt and pepper.

3. Put in the oven for 25–30 minutes, until the tomatoes are starting to blacken and are softened.

4. Process in a blender or food processor along with the stock, until smooth. Taste and adjust the seasoning, if necessary.

5. Serve each portion of soup drizzled with a little pesto and a pinch of pepper.

2

3

4

Chilled Avocado Soup

 SERVES 4    PREP TIME: 10 minutes    COOKING TIME: No cooking

nutritional information per serving	311 cal, 29g fat, 12g sat fat, 2g total sugars, 0.4g salt

On a hot day, this soup makes the perfect appetizer for a refreshing summer meal. Serve thoroughly chilled.

INGREDIENTS

2 avocados

1 tablespoon lemon juice

1 tablespoon snipped fresh chives, plus extra to garnish

1 tablespoon chopped fresh flat-leaf parsley

2 cups chicken stock, chilled

1¼ cups light cream, plus extra to serve

dash of Worcestershire sauce

salt and pepper, to taste

1. Halve the avocados and remove the pits. Scoop out the flesh and coarsely chop.

2. Put the avocado flesh, lemon juice, chives, parsley, stock, cream, and Worcestershire sauce in the blender and process until smooth. Season with salt and pepper.

3. Transfer the soup to a bowl, cover, and chill until required. Serve with light cream drizzled over the soup, topped with snipped chives.

Edamame Soup with Spinach & Basil

nutritional information per serving	323 cal, 12.5g fat, 2g sat fat, 6.5g total sugars, 1.4g salt

Edamame, or soybeans, are vibrant in color and packed with goodness. This soup is quick to prepare and perfect served with some crispy shards of lightly sautéed chorizo sausage.

INGREDIENTS

1 tablespoon vegetable oil

1 onion, finely chopped

2 cloves garlic, crushed

2 celery stalks, finely chopped

1⅔ cups shelled edamame

3 cups chicken stock

1 (6-ounce) package fresh spinach, trimmed and chopped

2 teaspoons finely chopped fresh basil

salt and pepper, to taste

coarsely grated Parmesan cheese, to serve

1. Heat the oil in a large saucepan over medium heat and sauté the onion, garlic, and celery for 4–5 minutes, until soft and golden.

2. Add the beans and stock, season with salt and pepper, then bring to a simmer, cover, and simmer for 12–15 minutes.

3. Add the spinach, replace the lid, and cook gently for 2–3 minutes, until the spinach has wilted completely.

4. Taste and adjust the seasoning, if necessary, then stir in the basil. Serve with Parmesan cheese sprinkled over the top.

2

3

4

COOK'S NOTE
If you can't find shelled edamame, buy frozen edamame (soybeans) instead— defrost and proceed as directed in the recipe.

Chile Chicken Soup

 SERVES 4  PREP TIME: 15 minutes  COOKING TIME: 25–30 minutes

nutritional information per serving	251 cal, 8g fat, 1.5g sat fat, 12g total sugars, 0.8g salt

This deliciously fresh and zingy soup produces an explosion of flavors on the palate. It has a light chile kick, which you can adjust to suit your taste.

INGREDIENTS

1 tablespoon vegetable oil

1 onion, finely chopped

2 celery stalks, finely chopped

2 carrots, finely chopped

1 red chile, seeded and finely chopped

2 cloves garlic, crushed

2 tablespoons tomato paste

1 tablespoon fresh oregano, finely chopped

2½ cups drained, canned whole tomatoes

2 cups chicken stock

2 skinless, boneless chicken breasts, cubed

juice of 1 lime

salt and pepper, to taste

to garnish

½ bunch scallions, finely chopped

½ avocado, peeled, pitted, and finely chopped

4 teaspoons chopped fresh cilantro

1. Heat the oil in a large saucepan and sauté the onion, celery, carrots, chile, and garlic and cook for 4–5 minutes.

2. Add the tomato paste and cook for an additional 1 minute, stirring continuously.

3. Add the oregano, tomatoes, and stock and bring to a gentle simmer, breaking down the tomatoes with the back of a wooden spoon to release the juices.

4. Add the chicken, season with salt and pepper, cover, and cook for an additional 20 minutes.

5. Remove from the heat, stir in the lime juice, and ladle the soup into serving bowls. Serve each portion topped with a selection of garnishes.

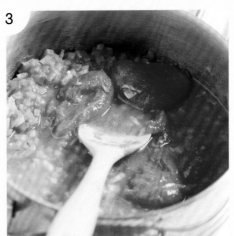

Ham & Black-Eyed Pea Soup

 SERVES 4

 PREP TIME:
10 minutes

 COOKING TIME:
35–40 minutes

nutritional information
per serving   174 cal, 5g fat, 1g sat fat, 8.5g total sugars, 1.1g salt

Enjoy this filling summer soup, perfectly suited to using up leftovers and pantry staples.

INGREDIENTS

1 tablespoon olive oil

1 onion, finely chopped

2 cloves garlic, finely chopped

2 celery stalks, finely chopped

1 teaspoon whole cumin seeds

2 teaspoons smoked paprika

1 (14½-ounce) can diced tomatoes

1 teaspoon Worcestershire sauce

1 tablespoon packed brown sugar

2 cups chicken stock

4 ounces cooked ham

1¼ cups drained, canned black-eyed peas

salt and pepper, to taste

fresh flat-leaf parsley, chopped

1. Heat the oil in a large saucepan and sauté the onion, garlic, and celery for 4–5 minutes, until softened.

2. Add the cumin and paprika and cook for an additional 1 minute, stirring continuously.

3. Add the tomatoes, Worcestershire sauce, sugar, and stock, and season with salt and pepper. Cover and simmer for 20 minutes, stirring occasionally. Meanwhile, coarsely chop the cooked ham.

4. Add the peas and ham and cook for an additional 5–10 minutes.

5. Adjust the seasoning, if necessary, stir in the parsley, and serve immediately.

SOMETHING DIFFERENT

If you want to make this vegetarian, simply use vegetable stock and omit the ham. Try other types of beans in the soup, such as navy or cranberry beans.

Lettuce & Arugula Soup

 SERVES 6    PREP TIME: 20 minutes    COOKING TIME: 50–55 minutes

nutritional information per serving	308 cal, 18.5g fat, 11g sat fat, 6g total sugars, 0.8g salt

Use a good-quality vegetable stock in this recipe and you will have a fantastic summery soup bursting with nutrients and packed with flavor. Rice gives the soup body and helps to make it more substantial.

INGREDIENTS

1 tablespoon butter

1 large onion, halved and sliced

2 leeks, sliced

6 cups vegetable stock

½ cup white rice

2 carrots, sliced

3 cloves garlic

1 bay leaf

2 butterhead lettuce (about 1 pound), cored and coarsely chopped

¾ cup heavy cream

freshly grated nutmeg

3 cups coarsely chopped arugula leaves, plus extra leaves to garnish

salt and pepper, to taste

1. Melt the butter in a large saucepan over medium heat and add the onion and leeks. Cover and cook, stirring frequently, for 3–4 minutes, until the vegetables begin to soften.

2. Add the stock, rice, carrots, garlic, and bay leaf with a large pinch of salt. Bring just to a boil, then reduce the heat, cover, and simmer for 25–30 minutes, or until the rice and vegetables are tender. Remove and discard the bay leaf.

3. Add the lettuce to the saucepan and cook, stirring occasionally, for 10 minutes, until the leaves are wilted.

4. Remove the saucepan from the heat and let cool slightly. Transfer to a food processor or blender, in batches if necessary, and process until smooth.

5. Return the soup to the rinsed-out pan and reheat gently; do not boil. Stir in the cream, reserving a little for the garnish, and add nutmeg to taste. Simmer, stirring occasionally, for 5 minutes, until warmed through.

6. Add the arugula leaves and simmer, stirring occasionally, for 2–3 minutes, until wilted. Taste and adjust the seasoning, adding salt and pepper if needed, and ladle the soup into warm bowls. Top each serving with a swirl of cream and a few arugula leaves and serve immediately.

Curried Zucchini Soup

 SERVES 4    PREP TIME: 10 minutes   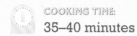 COOKING TIME: 35–40 minutes

nutritional information per serving	162 cal, 9.5g fat, 5.5g sat fat, 6.5g total sugars, 0.4g salt

Make this soup in the height of summer, when zucchini are most plentiful and cheap to buy. Adjust the strength of the curry flavor to your own personal taste.

INGREDIENTS

½ tablespoon butter

1 large onion, coarsely chopped

4–5 zucchini (about 2 pounds), sliced

2 cups vegetable stock

1 teaspoon curry powder

½ cup sour cream, plus extra to serve

salt and pepper

1. Melt the butter in a large saucepan over medium heat. Add the onion and cook for about 3 minutes, until beginning to soften.

2. Add the zucchini, stock, and curry powder, then season with salt. Bring the soup to a boil, then reduce the heat, cover, and cook gently for about 25 minutes, or until the vegetables are tender.

3. Remove the saucepan from the heat and let cool slightly. Transfer to a food processor or blender, in batches if necessary, and process until smooth.

4. Return the soup to the rinsed-out pan, stir in the sour cream, and reheat gently; do not boil.

5. Taste and adjust the seasoning, adding salt and pepper, if needed. Ladle into warm bowls, top each with a spoonful of sour cream, and serve immediately.

1

2

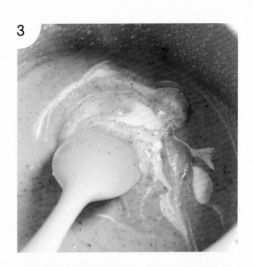

3

Southwest Vegetable Soup

 SERVES 6

 PREP TIME:
25 minutes

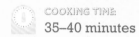 COOKING TIME:
35–40 minutes

nutritional information per serving	150 cal, 5g fat, 0.5g sat fat, 6g total sugars, 0.6g salt

More than just a soup, this is a big bowl bursting with the flavors and spices of the Southwest. It's a complete meal in a bowl, an explosion of big flavors and color, and all that in under an hour of cooking!

INGREDIENTS

2 tablespoons vegetable oil

1 onion, finely chopped

4 cloves garlic, finely chopped

¼–½ teaspoon ground cumin

2–3 teaspoons mild chili powder

1 carrot, sliced

1 Yukon gold, red-skinned, or white round potato, diced

3 fresh tomatoes, diced

1 zucchini, diced

¼ small head of cabbage, cored and finely shredded

about 4 cups vegetable stock or chicken stock

1 fresh corn cob or 2 cups corn kernels, thawed if frozen

10 green beans, cut into bite-size lengths

salt and pepper, to taste

chopped fresh cilantro and sliced fresh green chile, to garnish

tortilla chips, to serve

1. Heat the oil in a large saucepan over medium heat. Add the onion and garlic and cook for 3–4 minutes, until softened, then sprinkle in the cumin and chili powder. Stir in the carrot, potato, tomatoes, zucchini, and cabbage and cook, stirring occasionally, for 2 minutes.

2. Pour in the stock. Cover and cook over medium heat for 20 minutes, or until the vegetables are tender.

3. Meanwhile, remove and discard the husks and silks from the corn cob, then cut off the kernels, using a small sharp knife. Add a little extra stock to the soup, if needed, then stir in the corn kernels and beans and cook for an additional 5–10 minutes, or until the beans are tender. Season with salt and pepper.

4. Ladle the soup into warm bowls and garnish with cilantro and chile. Serve immediately with tortilla chips.

Avocado Soup
with Guacamole Toasts

 SERVES 6   PREP TIME: 15 minutes   COOKING TIME: 30–35 minutes

nutritional information per serving	476 cal, 39g fat, 15g sat fat, 3.5g total sugars, 1g salt

Cooking the avocado brings out it's buttery sweetness, which contrasts with the crispy texture of the toasts.

INGREDIENTS

3 ripe avocados

2 tablespoons lemon juice

6 tablespoons butter

6 shallots, chopped

1½ tablespoons all-purpose flour

3½ cups vegetable stock

¾ cup light cream

salt and pepper, to taste

extra virgin olive oil, for drizzling

1 lime, thinly sliced, to garnish

guacamole toasts

6 thin slices of day-old baguette

olive oil, for brushing

½ large ripe avocado, pitted and brushed with lime juice

juice of 1 lime

½ teaspoon hot pepper sauce, or to taste

1. Halve the avocados lengthwise and gently twist the halves apart. Remove and discard the pits and scoop out the flesh. Chop into small pieces, put them into a bowl, sprinkle with the lemon juice, and toss well to coat.

2. Melt the butter in a saucepan. Add the shallots and cook over low heat, stirring occasionally, for 5 minutes, until softened. Stir in the flour and cook, stirring continuously, for 1 minute. Remove the pan from the heat and gradually stir in the stock. Return the pan to medium heat and bring to a boil, stirring continuously.

3. Add the chopped avocado, reduce the heat, cover, and simmer for 15 minutes.

4. Meanwhile, to make the guacamole toasts, preheat the broiler. Toast the bread on one side under the preheated broiler. Turn the slices over, brush with oil, and toast the second side. Remove from the heat. Scoop out the avocado flesh into a bowl, mash with the lime juice and hot pepper sauce, and season with salt and pepper. Divide the avocado mixture among the toasts and set aside.

5. Remove the soup from the heat and push it through a strainer set over a bowl. Return the strained soup to the rinsed-out pan, stir in the cream, and reheat gently; do not boil. Season with salt and pepper.

6. Ladle the soup into warm bowls, drizzle with olive oil, and garnish with the lime slices. Serve with the guacamole toasts.

2

4

5

Salmon & Leek Soup

 SERVES 4    PREP TIME: 20 minutes    COOKING TIME: 40–45 minutes

nutritional information **per serving**   316 cal, 22g fat, 9g sat fat, 4g total sugars, 1.1g salt

This chowder like creamy soup is a delicious light bite—quick to cook and filled with tasty flavors.

INGREDIENTS

1 tablespoon olive oil

1 large onion, finely chopped

3 large leeks, including green parts, thinly sliced

1 potato, finely diced

2 cups fish stock

3 cups water

1 bay leaf

12 ounces skinless salmon fillet, cut into ½-inch cubes

⅓ cup heavy cream

lemon juice, to taste (optional)

salt and pepper, to taste

fresh flat-leaf parsley, to garnish

1. Heat the oil in a heavy saucepan over medium heat. Add the onion and leeks, and cook for about 3 minutes, until they begin to soften.

2. Add the potato, stock, water, and bay leaf with a large pinch of salt. Bring to a boil, then reduce the heat, cover, and cook gently for 25 minutes, or until the vegetables are tender. Remove and discard the bay leaf.

3. Remove the soup from the heat and let cool slightly. Transfer half the soup to a food processor or blender and process until smooth. Return the mixture to the pan with the rest of the soup and stir well.

4. Season the salmon with salt and pepper and add to the soup. Reheat gently, then cook for 5 minutes, or until the fish is cooked through and flakes easily. Stir in the cream, taste, and adjust the seasoning, adding a little lemon juice, if using. Ladle into warm bowls, garnish with parsley sprigs, and serve immediately.

2

3

4

SOMETHING
DIFFERENT
Swap the cubes of
salmon for another
firm white fish,
such as cod or
tilapia.

Chilled Fava Bean Soup

 SERVES 6    PREP TIME: 15 minutes    COOKING TIME: 10–15 minutes

nutritional information **per serving**	116 cal, 2.5g fat, 1g sat fat, 2g total sugars, 0.4g salt

This vibrant soup provides a wonderful contrast of flavors; the summer savory and mint give the soup a light, fresh flavor.

INGREDIENTS

3½ cups vegetable stock

2⅓ cups shelled fresh young fava beans

3 tablespoons lemon juice

2 tablespoons chopped fresh summer savory or fresh thyme

salt and pepper, to taste

6 tablespoons Greek-style yogurt, to serve

chopped fresh mint, to garnish

1. Pour the stock into a large saucepan and bring to a boil. Reduce the heat to a simmer, add the fava beans, and cook for about 7 minutes, or until the beans are tender.

2. Remove the pan from the heat and let cool slightly. Transfer to a food processor or blender, in batches if necessary, and process until smooth. Push the mixture through a strainer set over a bowl.

3. Stir in the lemon juice and summer savory and season with salt and pepper. Let cool completely, then cover with plastic wrap and chill in the refrigerator for at least 3 hours.

4. To serve, ladle into chilled bowls, top each with 1 tablespoon of yogurt, and garnish with mint. Serve immediately.

1

2

3

GOES WELL WITH
Serve with crispy
bread sticks or
lightly toasted
bread generously
spread with
garlic butter.

Asparagus Soup

 SERVES 6

 PREP TIME:
10 minutes

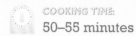 COOKING TIME:
50–55 minutes

nutritional information
per serving

240 cal, 16g fat, 10g sat fat, 5.5g total sugars, 0.6g salt

Best made at the height of the asparagus season, this fresh summer soup is completely delicious.

INGREDIENTS

1 bunch asparagus
(about 12 ounces)
3 cups vegetable stock
4 tablespoons butter
1 onion, chopped
3 tablespoons all-purpose flour
¼ teaspoon ground coriander
1 tablespoon lemon juice
2 cups milk
4–6 tablespoons heavy cream
or light cream
salt and pepper, to taste

1. Wash and trim the asparagus, discarding the woody part of the stem. Cut the remainder into short pieces, reserving the tips for garnish.

2. Cook the asparagus tips in ½ inch of boiling water for 5–10 minutes, or until tender. Drain and set aside.

3. Put the asparagus stems in a saucepan with the stock, then bring to a boil, cover, and simmer for about 20 minutes, or until the asparagus is soft. Drain and reserve the stock.

4. Melt the butter in a saucepan. Add the onion and cook over low heat for 3–4 minutes, or until soft. Stir in the flour and cook for 1 minute, then gradually whisk in the reserved stock and bring to a boil.

5. Simmer for 2–3 minutes, until thickened, then stir in the cooked asparagus stems, coriander, and lemon juice and season with salt and pepper. Simmer for 10 minutes. Remove the saucepan from the heat and let cool slightly. Transfer to a food processor or blender, in batches if necessary, and process until smooth.

6. Return the soup to the rinsed-out pan, add the milk and reserved asparagus tips, and bring to a boil. Simmer for 2 minutes. Stir in the cream and reheat gently; do not boil. Ladle into warm bowls and serve immediately.

Crab & Ginger Soup

 SERVES 4    PREP TIME: 10 minutes    COOKING TIME: 25–30 minutes

nutritional information per serving	363 cal, 16g fat, 5g sat fat, 6g total sugars, 1.7g salt

The rich crab meat is offset perfectly by the aromatic ginger, sweet coconut milk, and fresh lime juice and rind, making a delicious Thai-inspired soup.

INGREDIENTS

2 tablespoons chili oil

1 clove garlic, chopped

4 scallions, trimmed and sliced

2 red bell peppers, seeded and chopped

1 tablespoon grated fresh ginger

4 cups fish stock

3½ cups coconut milk

½ cup rice wine or sherry

2 tablespoons lime juice

1 tablespoon grated lime rind

6 young kaffir lime leaves, finely shredded

10 ounces freshly cooked crabmeat

8 ounces freshly cooked crab claws

1 cup drained, canned corn kernels

1 tablespoon chopped fresh cilantro, plus a few sprigs to garnish

salt and pepper, to taste

1. Heat the oil in a large saucepan over medium heat. Add the garlic and scallions and cook, stirring, for about 3 minutes, until slightly softened. Add the red bell peppers and ginger and cook for an additional 4 minutes, stirring.

2. Pour in the stock and season with salt and pepper. Bring to a boil, then reduce the heat. Pour in the coconut milk, rice wine, and lime juice, and stir in the grated lime rind and kaffir lime leaves. Simmer for 15 minutes.

3. Add the crabmeat and crab claws to the soup with the corn and cilantro. Cook the soup for 5 minutes, or until the crab is heated through.

4. Remove from the heat. Ladle into warm soup bowls, garnish with sprigs of cilantro, and serve immediately.

Summer Vegetable Soup with Pistou Sauce

 SERVES 6  PREP TIME: 20 minutes  COOKING TIME: 45–50 minutes

nutritional information per serving	120 cal, 2.5g fat, 1.5g sat fat, 6g total sugars, 0.5g salt

Pistou sauce is similar to pesto but without the pine nuts. Stirred into this punchy vegetable soup, it provides a fantastic hit of flavor.

INGREDIENTS

4 tomatoes, peeled, seeded, and diced

¾ cup bite-size green bean pieces

1 fennel bulb, quartered and sliced

1 carrot, diced

1 zucchini, diced

1 bouquet garni (fresh flat-leaf parsley, thyme sprigs, and a bay leaf tied together)

pinch of sugar

2 tablespoons tomato paste

½ cup shelled fava beans or shelled peas

1 (15-ounce) can navy beans, drained and rinsed

2 tablespoons dried soup pasta

salt and pepper, to taste

pistou sauce

3 cloves garlic, coarsely chopped

1¼ cups basil leaves

⅓ cup grated Parmesan cheese

⅓ cup extra virgin olive oil

1. Put the tomatoes, green beans, fennel, carrot, zucchini, bouquet garni, sugar, and tomato paste into a large, heavy saucepan. Pour in enough water to cover the vegetables by 3 inches and season generously with salt and pepper. Cover the pan and bring to a boil, then stir well, reduce the heat, and simmer for 40–45 minutes, or until the vegetables are tender.

2. Meanwhile, to make the pistou sauce, crush the garlic in a large mortar. Add the basil, Parmesan cheese, and salt and use the pestle to grind together to form a rough paste. Stir in the oil, 1 tablespoon at a time, then transfer to a bowl and set aside.

3. Uncover the soup and increase the heat to a slow boil. Add the fava beans and navy beans and boil for 5–10 minutes, or until the beans are tender. Add the pasta and cook according to the package directions, until the pasta is tender but still firm to the bite. The soup should be chunky, but stir in extra water with the beans if too much liquid has evaporated.

4. Remove and discard the bouquet garni. Stir in the pistou sauce. Taste and adjust the seasoning with salt and pepper, if necessary. Serve immediately.

Potato & Pesto Soup

 SERVES 4    PREP TIME: 20 minutes    COOKING TIME: 40–45 minutes

nutritional information per serving	1076 cal, 83g fat, 29g sat fat, 15g total sugars, 1.6g salt

Creamy potatoes and pasta contrast wonderfully with homemade pesto to make a fresh-tasting, filling soup.

INGREDIENTS

2 tablespoons olive oil

3 rindless bacon strips, finely chopped

2 tablespoons butter

4 Yukon gold, red-skinned, or white round potatoes, chopped

3 onions, finely chopped

2½ cups chicken stock

2½ cups milk

4 ounces dried conchigliette (small pasta shells)

⅔ cup heavy cream

2 tablespoons chopped fresh parsley

salt and pepper, to taste

pesto

1 cup finely chopped fresh parsley

2 cloves garlic, crushed

⅓ cup pine nuts, crushed

2 tablespoons chopped fresh basil leaves

⅔ cup freshly grated Parmesan cheese, plus extra to serve

⅔ cup olive oil

white pepper, to taste

1. To make the pesto, put all of the ingredients in a food processor or blender and process for 2 minutes to form a coarse paste. Scrape into a small bowl and set aside.

2. Heat the oil in a large saucepan and cook the bacon over medium heat for 4 minutes. Add the butter, potatoes, and onions and cook, stirring continuously, for 12 minutes.

3. Add the stock and milk to the saucepan, bring to a boil, and simmer for 10 minutes. Add the pasta and simmer for an additional 3–4 minutes.

4. Stir in the cream and simmer for 5 minutes. Add the parsley, season with salt and pepper, and stir in 2 tablespoons of the pesto. Ladle the soup into warm bowls, sprinkle with Parmesan cheese, and serve immediately.

1

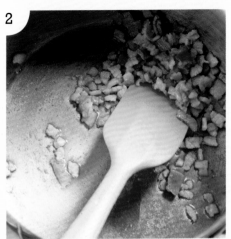

2

3

Pea Soup

nutritional information per serving	274 cal, 16g fat, 10g sat fat, 3.5g total sugars, 0.9g salt

Peas are the essence of summer, and their sweet flavor works well in soup. Topped with crumbled Roquefort and crispy croutons, this is a mouthwatering delight.

INGREDIENTS

3 tablespoons butter

¼ cup finely chopped shallots

4 cups vegetable stock or water

3 cups shelled peas

pinch of sugar

¼ cup crème fraîche or Greek yogurt

salt and pepper, to taste

croutons and blue cheese, such as Roquefort, crumbled, to serve

1. Melt the butter in a large saucepan over medium heat. Add the shallots and sauté for 2–3 minutes, or until soft. Add the stock, peas, and sugar, season with salt and pepper, and bring to a boil, uncovered. Simmer for 15–20 minutes, or until the peas are tender.

2. Strain the peas and reserve the cooking liquid. Process the peas in a food processor or blender, until smooth, then return the puree to the pan. Gradually stir in the cooking liquid until you have the desired consistency.

3. Reheat the soup; do not boil. Stir in the crème fraîche or yogurt and adjust the seasoning, if necessary. Serve immediately with blue cheese and croutons sprinkled over the soup.

1

2

2

COOK'S NOTE
Use either frozen or freshly shelled peas in this recipe. If preferred, swap the Roquefort for a milder blue cheese, such as Stilton.

Chilled Red Pepper Soup

 SERVES 6

 PREP TIME:
15 minutes
plus chilling

COOKING TIME:
50–55 minutes

nutritional information per serving	272 cal, 14g fat, 2.5g sat fat, 11.5g total sugars, 0.8g salt

Roasting the red bell peppers adds a natural sweetness to this recipe—serve with salted croutons to balance the flavors.

INGREDIENTS

3 red bell peppers
3 tablespoons olive oil
1 Spanish onion, chopped
3 cloves garlic, finely chopped
9 ripe tomatoes (about 2¼ pounds), peeled, seeded, and coarsely chopped
⅓ cup red wine
1 teaspoon sugar
4 cups vegetable stock
salt and pepper, to taste
chili oil, for drizzling
croutons, to serve

1. Preheat the broiler to high. Put the bell peppers on a baking sheet and broil, turning frequently, for 10 minutes, until the skins are charred. Remove with tongs, put them into a plastic bag, seal, and let cool. Peel off the skins, halve, and seed, then coarsely chop the flesh.

2. Heat the oil in a large saucepan. Add the onion and garlic and cook over low heat, stirring occasionally, for 5 minutes, until softened. Add the red peppers and tomatoes, stir well, cover, and cook, stirring occasionally, for 8–10 minutes.

3. Increase the heat to medium, pour in the wine, and cook for 2 minutes, or until the alcohol has evaporated. Stir in the sugar, pour in the stock, and bring to a boil. Season with salt and pepper, then reduce the heat and simmer for 30 minutes.

4. Remove the pan from the heat and let cool slightly. Transfer to a food processor or blender and process until smooth, then transfer to a bowl and let cool completely. Cover with plastic wrap and chill in the refrigerator for at least 3 hours.

5. Ladle the soup into bowls, drizzle with chili oil, sprinkle with croutons, and serve immediately.

Hot & Sour Soup
with Salmon

 SERVES 4

 PREP TIME:
20 minutes

 COOKING TIME:
25–30 minutes

nutritional information
per serving | 193 cal, 8g fat, 1.5g sat fat, 2g total sugars, 2.2g salt

Not only is this a great restorative soup that is low in fat and high in nutrients, but it's delicious, too.

INGREDIENTS

8 ounces skinless salmon fillet,

2 teaspoons sesame oil

4 cups vegetable stock

1 cup fresh cilantro, stems and leaves separated

2 Thai chiles, halved lengthwise

1 lemongrass stalk, coarsely chopped

3½ cups quartered cremini mushrooms,

2 tablespoons Thai fish sauce

1 cup diagonally sliced snow peas

4 scallions, thinly sliced

finely grated zest and juice of 2 limes

1. Preheat the broiler to high. Cut the salmon into several pieces and put on an aluminum foil-lined broiler pan. Brush the fish lightly with the sesame oil, then broil for 3–4 minutes, until almost cooked through. Flake into bite-size pieces and set aside.

2. Pour the stock into a large saucepan. Add the cilantro stems, chiles, and lemongrass. Bring to a boil, cover, and simmer for 5 minutes. Push through a strainer into a bowl, remove and discard the flavorings, and return the stock to the pan.

3. Add the mushrooms and fish sauce to the pan. Cover and simmer for 3 minutes. Meanwhile, shred half the cilantro leaves.

4. Add the snow peas, scallions, shredded cilantro leaves, salmon, and lime zest to the pan and reheat gently; do not boil. Stir in the lime juice to taste. Ladle into warm bowls, sprinkle with the remaining cilantro leaves, and serve immediately.

1

2

3

BE PREPARED *Precook the salmon, cover, and chill until required.*

Chicken, Avocado
& Chipotle Soup

 SERVES 6    PREP TIME: 10 minutes   COOKING TIME: 5 minutes

nutritional information per serving	166 cal, 5.5g fat, 1.5g sat fat, 0.3g total sugars, 0.8g salt

This light but spicy chicken broth is a perfect lunchtime bite for hot summer days.

INGREDIENTS

6 cups chicken stock

2–3 cloves garlic, finely chopped

1–2 dried chipotle chiles, thinly sliced

1 avocado

juice of ½ lime

3–5 scallions, thinly sliced

2½–3 cups bite-size, torn cooked chicken breast

2 tablespoons chopped fresh cilantro

1 lime, cut into wedges, to serve

1. Put the stock in a large saucepan with the garlic and chiles and bring to a boil.

2. Meanwhile, cut the avocado in half around the pit. Twist apart, then remove the pit with a knife. Remove and discard the skin, dice the flesh, and toss in the lime juice to prevent discoloration.

3. Arrange the scallions, chicken, avocado, and cilantro in warm bowls.

4. Ladle hot stock over the bowls' contents and serve immediately with lime wedges.

1

2

2

GOES WELL WITH
Serve with lightly
salted tortilla
chips—they
are the perfect
antidote to the
heat of the chile.

Chicken & Lemon Soup

 SERVES 4

 PREP TIME:
15 minutes

 COOKING TIME:
50–55 minutes

nutritional information per serving	646 cal, 34.5g fat, 20.5g sat fat, 7g total sugars, 1.3g salt

A soup that captures summer in a bowl, with tasty vegetables and a refreshing zingy flavor.

INGREDIENTS

4 tablespoons butter

8 shallots, thinly sliced

2 carrots, thinly sliced

2 celery stalks, thinly sliced

8 ounces skinless, boneless chicken breasts, finely chopped

3 lemons

5 cups chicken stock

8 ounces dried spaghetti, broken into small pieces

⅔ cup heavy cream

salt and pepper, to taste

2 lemon slices, halved, to garnish

1. Melt the butter in a large saucepan. Add the shallots, carrots, celery, and chicken and cook over low heat, stirring occasionally, for 5 minutes.

2. Thinly pare the lemons and blanch the lemon rind in boiling water for 3 minutes. Squeeze the juice from the lemon and reserve.

3. Add the lemon rind and juice to the saucepan, along with the stock. Bring the soup to a boil, then reduce the heat and simmer for 40 minutes, stirring occasionally.

4. Add the spaghetti to the saucepan and cook according to the package directions, until the spaghetti is tender and the chicken is cooked through. Season with salt and pepper and add the cream. Heat through gently; do not let the soup boil.

5. Ladle into warm bowls, garnish with slices of lemon, and serve immediately.

1

2

3

Chicken & Collard Greens Soup

 SERVES 4

 PREP TIME:
20 minutes

 COOKING TIME:
15–20 minutes

nutritional information per serving	293 cal, 7.5g fat, 1.5g sat fat, 6.5g total sugars, 1.6g salt

Show off the best of summer's produce with this nourishing soup that is satisfying without being heavy. A great way to help use the best vegetables of the season.

INGREDIENTS

2 tablespoons olive oil

2 skinless chicken breasts, thinly sliced

2 cloves garlic, crushed

2 zucchini, cut into large dice

2 cups green bean pieces

3 tomatoes, seeded and coarsely chopped

1 (15-ounce) can pinto beans, drained and rinsed

5 cups vegetable stock

12 fresh basil leaves, chopped

pepper, to taste

1. Heat the oil in a large saucepan set over medium heat. Add the chicken and garlic and cook, stirring, for 3 minutes; do not let the chicken or garlic brown.

2. Stir in the zucchini, green beans, tomatoes, pinto beans, and stock. Cover and simmer for 10–12 minutes, or until the chicken is cooked through and the vegetables are tender.

3. Stir in the basil leaves and season with pepper. Ladle into warm bowls and serve immediately.

GOES WELL WITH
To make Parmesan
chips, cook
2-inch diameter
disks of grated
Parmesan cheese
on a lined bak-
ing sheet in a
preheated oven,
at 325°F, until
melted and golden
brown.

White Bean Soup

 SERVES 4

 PREP TIME:
10 minutes
plus soaking

 COOKING TIME:
2¼–2½ hours

nutritional information per serving	456 cal, 18g fat, 2.5g sat fat, 2g total sugars, 1.1g salt

Beans are a wonderful pantry standby for bulking out soups, and they're a healthy addition to any meal.

INGREDIENTS

1 cup dried cannellini beans, soaked overnight or for at least 5 hours

6 cups vegetable stock

4 ounces dried soup pasta

⅓ cup olive oil

2 cloves garlic, finely chopped

¼ cup chopped fresh flat-leaf parsley

salt and pepper, to taste

1. Drain and rinse the beans and put them in a large saucepan. Add the stock and bring to a boil. Partly cover the pan, then reduce the heat and simmer for 2 hours, or until tender.

2. Transfer half the beans and a little of the stock to a food processor or blender and process until smooth. Return the mixture to the pan and stir well to mix. Gently return the soup to a boil.

3. Add the pasta, bring back to a boil, and cook according to the package directions, until the pasta is tender.

4. Meanwhile, heat ¼ cup of the olive oil in a small saucepan. Add the garlic and cook over low heat, stirring frequently, for 4–5 minutes, or until golden. Stir the garlic mixture into the soup and add the parsley. Season with salt and pepper and ladle into warm bowls. Drizzle with the remaining olive oil and serve immediately.

1

2

3

COOK'S NOTE

Save time soaking the beans by using canned beans instead. Simply drain and cook as per the directions in step 2.

Chilled Pea Soup

 SERVES 4

 PREP TIME:
15 minutes
plus chilling

 COOKING TIME:
10 minutes

nutritional information per serving	210 cal, 7g fat, 2.5g sat fat, 10g total sugars, 0.5g salt

This soup is ideal for entertaining because it can be made and chilled, ready for the arrival of guests.

INGREDIENTS

2 cups vegetable stock or water
3 cups frozen peas
4 scallions, coarsely chopped
1¼ cups plain yogurt
salt and pepper, to taste

to garnish
2 tablespoons chopped fresh mint
2 tablespoons chopped scallions or chives
grated lemon rind
olive oil

1. Bring the stock to a boil in a large saucepan over medium heat. Reduce the heat, add the peas and scallions, and simmer for 5 minutes.

2. Let cool slightly, then push through a strainer into a bowl. Season with salt and pepper and stir in the yogurt. Cover the bowl with plastic wrap and chill in the refrigerator for several hours, or until well chilled.

3. To serve, remove from the refrigerator, mix well, and ladle into chilled serving bowls. Garnish with the chopped mint, scallions, grated lemon rind, and olive oil.

1

2

2

GOES WELL WITH
Make your own melba toast. Lightly toast a piece of sliced bread, then slice it in half again horizontally, and lightly toast once more so that all the edges are crisp. Cut into triangles to serve.

Chilled Melon Soup

 SERVES 4

 PREP TIME:
10 minutes

COOKING TIME:
No cooking

nutritional information per serving	55 cal, 0g fat, 0g sat fat, 11.5g total sugars, trace salt

Serve this super fresh, sweet juicy soup ice cold from the refrigerator. It's wonderful on a sunny day with a salad to follow, or served between courses in frosted shot glasses for real impact!

INGREDIENTS

1 sweet ripe cantaloupe

½ cup fresh orange juice

2 tablespoons finely chopped fresh basil, plus a little extra to garnish

several handfuls ice

pepper, to taste

1. Peel the melon, scoop out the seeds, and discard and cut the flesh into small cubes.

2. Put the melon flesh in a food processor or blender, along with the orange juice, basil, and ice.

3. Process until smooth and serve immediately, garnished with the extra basil and pepper.

Scallop Chowder *118*

Spiced Winter Squash Soup *120*

Cream of Mushroom Soup *122*

Chicken & Mushroom Soup with Puff Pastry *124*

Spicy Lentil & Carrot Soup *126*

Italian Meatball Soup *128*

Beef & Cabbage Soup *130*

Curried Vegetable Soup *132*

Jerusalem Artichoke Soup *134*

Sauerkraut & Sausage Soup *136*

Mixed Bean Soup with Gruyère *138*

Chestnut & Pancetta Soup *140*

Beef & Barley Broth *142*

Roasted Squash, Garlic & Thyme Soup *144*

Green Lentil & Vegetable Soup *146*

Carrot & Coriander Soup *148*

Split Pea & Ham Soup *150*

Barley, Lentil & Onion Soup *152*

Broccoli & Stilton Soup *154*

Vegetable & Corn Chowder *156*

Cheese & Bacon Soup *158*

Chicken Noodle Soup *160*

Butternut Squash & Smoky Bacon Soup *162*

Roasted Sweet Potato & Garlic Soup *164*

Winter Warmers

Scallop Chowder

 SERVES 6  PREP TIME: 15 minutes  COOKING TIME: 25–30 minutes

nutritional information per serving	358 cal, 15g fat, 8g sat fat, 8g total sugars, 1.8g salt

The ultimate in luxury comfort food—tasty fresh seafood combined with a silky vegetable broth, bursting with goodness and wonderfully satisfying.

INGREDIENTS

4 tablespoons butter

8 ounces large scallops, quartered

4 bacon strips, chopped

1 large onion, chopped

2 celery stalks, diced

2 carrots, diced

3 floury potatoes, diced

2 fresh thyme sprigs

3 tablespoons chopped fresh parsley

2 cups chicken stock or vegetable stock

2 cups milk, hot

8 ounces mixed cooked seafood, such as shrimp and mussels

squeeze of lemon juice

salt and pepper, to taste

1. Melt the butter in a large saucepan over medium heat. When it foams, add the scallops and cook, in batches, for 5 minutes, until lightly browned. Remove from the pan and set aside.

2. Add the bacon to the pan and cook for 3–4 minutes, until it starts to brown.

3. Add the onion, celery, carrots, and potatoes. Season with salt and pepper, then cover and cook over medium–low heat, stirring occasionally.

4. Add the thyme and 2 tablespoons of the parsley to the pan of vegetables. Pour in the stock, cover, and bring to a boil. Reduce the heat and simmer for 15 minutes, until the vegetables are soft.

5. Remove and discard the thyme sprigs. Lightly crush some of the vegetables with the back of a wooden spoon to thicken the liquid. Pour in the hot milk.

6. Add the scallops and mixed seafood to the pan. Cook until heated through but without letting the mixture boil. Check the seasoning, and add a squeeze of lemon juice. Ladle into warm bowls and serve sprinkled with the remaining parsley.

Spiced Winter Squash Soup

 SERVES 4

 PREP TIME:
20 minutes

 COOKING TIME:
35–40 minutes

nutritional information **per serving** | 125 cal, 6g fat, 1g sat fat, 5.5g total sugars, 0.4g salt

The perfect use for your Halloween pumpkin—scoop out the flesh and carve the tough outer left behind.

INGREDIENTS

2 tablespoons olive oil

1 onion, chopped

1 clove garlic, chopped

1 tablespoon chopped fresh ginger

1 small red chile, seeded and finely chopped

2 tablespoons chopped fresh cilantro, plus extra to garnish

1 bay leaf

8 cups peeled, seeded, and diced pumpkin or other winter squash, or 1 butternut squash, peeled, seeded, and diced

2½ cups vegetable stock

salt and pepper, to taste

light cream, to garnish

1. Heat the oil in a large saucepan over medium heat. Add the onion and garlic and cook for about 4 minutes, until slightly softened. Add the ginger, chile, cilantro, bay leaf, and squash and cook for an additional 3 minutes.

2. Pour in the stock and bring to a boil. Skim any foam from the surface, if necessary. Reduce the heat and simmer, stirring occasionally, for about 25 minutes, or until the pumpkin is tender. Remove from the heat, remove and discard the bay leaf, and let cool.

3. Transfer to a food processor or blender, in batches if necessary, and process until smooth. Return the mixture to the rinsed-out pan and season with salt and pepper.

4. Reheat gently, then remove from the heat and pour into warm soup bowls. Garnish each bowl with a swirl of cream and the cilantro, then serve.

COOK'S NOTE

Don't discard the pumpkin seeds—simply rinse and dry, then put onto a lined baking sheet and toss with oil and salt. Cook in a preheated oven at 275°F for 15 minutes, until golden brown.

Cream of Mushroom Soup

 SERVES 4    PREP TIME: 10 minutes   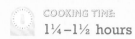 COOKING TIME: 1¼–1½ hours

nutritional information per serving	600 cal, 55g fat, 34.5g sat fat, 3g total sugars, 0.7g salt

The secret to this delicious soup is patience. The longer you cook and caramelize the mushrooms in the butter, the deeper and "meatier" the flavor will be. Take your time and you'll be richly rewarded.

INGREDIENTS

1 stick unsalted butter

13 cups thickly sliced white button mushrooms (about 2 pounds)

1 onion, coarsely chopped

1 tablespoon flour

4 cups chicken stock

1 cup water

6 sprigs fresh thyme, plus picked leaves to garnish

3 cloves garlic

1 cup heavy cream

salt and pepper, to taste

1. Melt the butter in a large saucepan over medium heat. Add the mushrooms and a pinch of salt. Cook, stirring occasionally, for 20–30 minutes, or until the mushrooms are golden brown. Reserve some of the browned mushrooms to garnish the soup later on.

2. Add the onions and cook over medium–low heat for about 5 minutes. Add the flour and cook, stirring, for 1 minute. Whisk in the stock and water. Add the thyme and garlic and bring to a simmer. Reduce the heat to low, cover, and simmer gently for 1 hour.

3. Remove the soup from the heat, uncover, and let cool for 15 minutes. Transfer to a food processor or blender, in batches if necessary, and process until smooth.

4. Return the soup to the rinsed-out pan and gently reheat; do not boil. Add the cream and adjust the seasoning, if necessary. Serve hot, topped with the reserved mushrooms and thyme leaves.

1

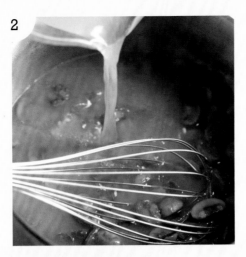

2

4

Chicken & Mushroom Soup with Puff Pastry

SERVES 4

PREP TIME:
10 minutes

COOKING TIME:
1–1¼ hours

nutritional information per serving	716 cal, 37g fat, 18.5g sat fat, 4g total sugars, 1.8g salt

The base of this soup is an mixture of cider and chicken stock that's delicious with the pastry top.

INGREDIENTS

2 chicken legs, skin removed

4 cups chicken stock

⅔ cup apple cider or apple juice

1 onion, finely chopped

1 bay leaf

4 cups thickly sliced cremini mushrooms

¼ cup cornstarch blended with ¼ cup water

¼ cup crème fraîche or heavy cream

salt and pepper, to taste

flour for sprinkling

1 sheet ready-to-bake puff pastry

1. Put the chicken legs in a large saucepan with the stock, cider or juice, onion, and bay leaf. Cover and simmer for 25 minutes. Add the mushrooms and simmer for an additional 10 minutes. Remove the chicken and set aside. Remove and discard the bay leaf.

2. Stir the cornstarch into the stock. Heat, stirring continuously, until boiling and thickened. Remove from the heat and let cool. Remove the meat from the chicken legs and tear into pieces.

3. Preheat the oven to 400°F. Stir the chicken and crème fraîche or heavy cream into the soup. Season with salt and pepper, then ladle into ovenproof bowls. They should be about three-quarters full.

4. Lightly flour a surface, then roll out the pastry. Cut out circles or squares large enough to cover the tops of the bowls with a ½-inch overlap. Brush the rim of each bowl with water, lay the pastry on top, press around the rim, and pierce the centers. Bake in the preheated oven for 20–25 minutes, or until the pastry is golden. Serve immediately.

1
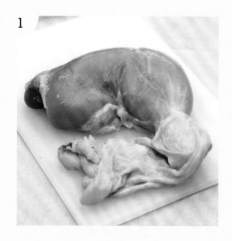

1

4

Spicy Lentil & Carrot Soup

 SERVES 4    PREP TIME: 15 minutes   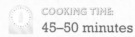 COOKING TIME: 45–50 minutes

nutritional information per serving	322 cal, 9g fat, 3g sat fat, 14g total sugars, 1g salt

Red lentils are a good source of protein and the perfect vessel for strong spicy flavors.

INGREDIENTS

⅔ cup dried split red lentils

5 cups vegetable stock

6 carrots, sliced

2 onions, chopped

1 cup canned diced tomatoes

2 cloves garlic, chopped

2 tablespoons oil

1 teaspoon ground cumin

1 teaspoon ground coriander

1 fresh green chile, seeded and chopped

½ teaspoon ground turmeric

1 tablespoon lemon juice

1¼ cups milk

2 tablespoons chopped fresh cilantro

salt and pepper, to taste

plain yogurt, to serve

1. Put the lentils in a large saucepan, along with 3½ cups of the stock, the carrots, onions, tomatoes, and garlic. Bring the mixture to a boil, then reduce the heat, cover, and simmer for 30 minutes, or until the vegetables and lentils are tender.

2. Meanwhile, heat the oil in a separate saucepan. Add the cumin, ground coriander, chile, and turmeric and sauté over low heat for 1 minute. Remove from the heat and stir in the lemon juice. Season with salt.

3. Remove the soup from the heat and let cool slightly. Transfer to a food processor or blender, in batches if necessary, and process until smooth. Return the soup to the rinsed-out pan, add the spice mixture and the remaining stock, and simmer over low heat for 10 minutes.

4. Add the milk and season with salt and pepper, if needed. Stir in the chopped cilantro and reheat gently; do not boil. Ladle into warm bowls, top each with a swirl of yogurt, and serve immediately.

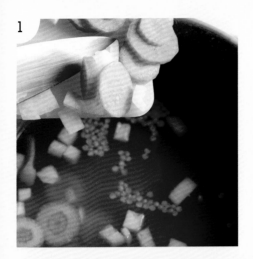

Italian Meatball Soup

SERVES 6

PREP TIME: 10 minutes

COOKING TIME: 25–30 minutes

nutritional information
per serving | 260 cal, 9g fat, 4g sat fat, 1g total sugars, 1.5g salt

A delicious broth with meatballs and mini pasta, this is made into a complete meal with the addition of the greens.

INGREDIENTS

12 ounces ground round or ground sirloin beef

¼ cup finely grated onion

2 tablespoons freshly grated Parmesan cheese, plus extra to serve

½ teaspoon pepper, or to taste

¼ teaspoon salt, or to taste

1 medium egg, beaten

8½ cups chicken stock,

2 ounces dried soup pasta

3¾ cups trimmed and finely shredded Swiss chard or savoy cabbage

1. Preheat the oven to 450°F.

2. Combine the beef, onion, Parmesan, ½ teaspoon of pepper, and ¼ teaspoon of salt in a bowl, mixing well with a fork. Stir in the beaten egg. Shape into 24 walnut-size balls and place on a nonstick baking sheet. Cook in the preheated oven for 5–7 minutes, turning once, until lightly browned. Remove from the oven and set aside.

3. Bring the stock to a boil in a large saucepan. Add the pasta and meatballs, then let simmer for 10 minutes.

4. Meanwhile, steam the Swiss chard for 2–3 minutes, until wilted. Transfer to a strainer and squeeze out as much liquid as possible, pressing with the back of a wooden spoon. Add the Swiss chard to the soup and cook for 5 minutes, or until the greens and pasta are tender.

5. Taste and season with salt and pepper, if needed. Ladle the soup into warm bowls and serve immediately with Parmesan.

2

3

4

Beef & Cabbage Soup

 SERVES 6    PREP TIME: 25 minutes    COOKING TIME: 50–55 minutes

nutritional information
per serving   254 cal, 4g fat, 0.5g sat fat, 5g total sugars, 0.7g salt

This is a warming and nourishing bowl of soup—using the best of winter produce to make a meal hearty enough to leave you feeling contented.

INGREDIENTS

2 tablespoons vegetable oil

1 onion, finely chopped

2 celery stalks, diced

2 carrots, diced

1 clove garlic, finely chopped

¼ teaspoon pepper, or to taste

6 cups beef stock

1 large potato, diced

2 cups cooked corned beef, brisket, bottom round roast, or rump roast cubes

2 cups shredded green cabbage

salt and pepper, to taste

3 tablespoons coarsely chopped fresh flat-leaf parsley, to garnish

1. Heat the oil in a large saucepan over medium heat. Add the onion, celery, and carrots, then cover and cook, stirring occasionally, for 5–7 minutes. Add the garlic and ¼ teaspoon of pepper and season with salt, then cook for an additional minute.

2. Pour in the stock and bring to a boil. Add the potato and beef, then simmer, partly covered, for 30 minutes.

3. Add the cabbage and bring back to a boil. Reduce the heat and simmer for an additional 15 minutes, or until the cabbage is tender.

4. Adjust the seasoning, adding salt and pepper, if needed. Ladle into warm bowls, garnish with the parsley, and serve immediately.

1

2

3

COOK'S NOTE

This recipe calls for corned beef, brisket, bottom round roast, or rump roast—all are economical cuts suited to gentle cooking to bring out a full flavor.

Curried Vegetable Soup

 SERVES 6    PREP TIME: 15 minutes    COOKING TIME: 45–50 minutes

nutritional information per serving	323 cal, 18g fat, 9g sat fat, 16g total sugars, 0.7g salt

Here is a smooth and creamy soup with wonderful flavors provided by aromatic spices and root vegetables— the addition of the lightly fried ginger as a garnish makes a great contrast.

INGREDIENTS

3 tablespoons butter
2 onions, chopped
2 cloves garlic, chopped
1½ teaspoons ground cumin
1 teaspoon ground coriander
1 sweet potato, chopped
2 carrots, chopped
3 parsnips, chopped
1 tablespoon curry paste
3 cups vegetable stock
3 cups milk
1 teaspoon lime juice
⅓ cup sour cream
salt and pepper, to taste

to garnish
4-inch piece of fresh ginger
2 tablespoons peanut oil

1. Melt the butter in a large saucepan. Add the onions and garlic and cook over low heat, stirring occasionally, for 8–10 minutes, until lightly browned. Stir in the cumin and coriander and cook, stirring continuously, for 2 minutes. Add the sweet potato, carrots, and parsnips and cook, stirring frequently, for 5 minutes, then stir in the curry paste and mix well. Increase the heat to medium, pour in the stock, and bring to a boil, stirring occasionally. Reduce the heat, cover, and simmer for 20–25 minutes, until the vegetables are tender.

2. Meanwhile, make the garnish. Cut the ginger in half and then into thin julienne strips. Heat the oil in a small skillet over high heat. Reduce the heat, add the ginger, and cook, stirring continuously, for 1 minute. Remove with a slotted spoon and drain on paper towels.

3. Remove the pan of soup from the heat and let cool slightly. Transfer to a food processor or blender, in batches if necessary, and process until smooth.

4. Return the soup to the rinsed-out pan and stir in the milk. Cook, stirring occasionally, for 5 minutes. Stir in the lime juice and 3 tablespoons of the sour cream and season with salt and pepper.

5. Ladle the soup into warm bowls, add a swirl of the remaining sour cream, and garnish with the fried ginger. Serve immediately.

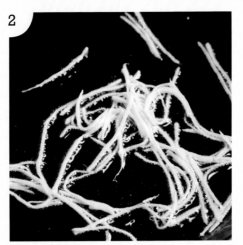

Jerusalem Artichoke Soup

 SERVES 6

 PREP TIME:
10 minutes

 COOKING TIME:
45–50 minutes

nutritional information per serving	306 cal, 21.5g fat, 11.5g sat fat, 4.5g total sugars, 0.8g salt

Jerusalem artichokes lend themselves perfectly to this velvety soup because they break down quickly and easily. Their sweet nutty flavor is delicious with the tangy chives, making a wonderfully comforting winter treat.

INGREDIENTS

1 tablespoon lemon juice
1½ pounds Jerusalem artichokes
4 tablespoons butter
1 tablespoon sunflower oil
1 onion, chopped
5½ cups vegetable stock
¾ cup milk
1 tablespoon snipped fresh chives, plus extra to garnish
½ cup heavy cream
salt and pepper, to taste
extra virgin olive oil, for drizzling
croutons, to serve

1. Fill a bowl with water and stir in the lemon juice. Peel the artichokes and cut into chunks, then immediately drop them into the water to prevent discoloration.

2. Heat the butter with the sunflower oil in a large saucepan. Add the onion and cook over low heat, stirring occasionally, for 5 minutes, until softened. Drain the artichokes, add them to the pan, and stir well. Cover and cook, stirring occasionally, for 15 minutes.

3. Pour in the stock and milk, increase the heat to medium, and bring to a boil. Reduce the heat, replace the lid, and simmer for 20 minutes, until the artichokes are soft.

4. Remove the pan from the heat and let cool slightly. Add the chives and transfer the soup to a food processor or blender, in batches if necessary, and process until smooth.

5. Return the soup to the rinsed-out pan, stir in the cream, and season with salt and pepper. Reheat gently, then ladle into warm bowls, drizzle with extra virgin olive oil, and serve immediately with croutons and chives

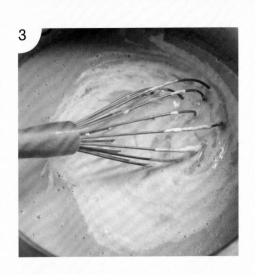

Sauerkraut & Sausage Soup

 SERVES 6    PREP TIME: 10 minutes    COOKING TIME: 35–40 minutes

nutritional information per serving	440 cal, 26g fat, 11.5g sat fat, 3.5g total sugars, 4.6g salt

This German-influenced dish is much more than a soup, with its chunks of cooked pork sausages and dumplings. It's both quick to prepare and plenty to feed and fill a whole family

INGREDIENTS

2 tablespoons butter

1 tablespoon all-purpose flour

1 tablespoon sweet paprika

8½ cups vegetable stock

3 cups drained sauerkraut

1 pound cooked smoked pork sausages, cut into 1-inch slices

⅔ cup sour cream

salt and pepper, to taste

dumplings

⅔ cup white bread flour, plus extra for dusting

pinch of salt

1 extra-large egg

1. Melt the butter in a large saucepan over low heat. Add the flour and paprika and cook, stirring continuously, for 2 minutes, then remove the pan from the heat. Gradually stir in the stock, a little at a time, until completely incorporated and the mixture is smooth.

2. Return the pan to medium heat and bring to a boil, stirring continuously. Add the sauerkraut and sausages and season with salt and pepper. Reduce the heat, cover, and simmer for 30 minutes.

3. Meanwhile, make the dumplings. Sift the flour and salt into a bowl. Beat the egg in a separate bowl, then gradually beat in the dry ingredients, a little at a time. Turn out onto a floured surface and knead until smooth. Cover and let rest for 15 minutes.

4. Divide the dough into six pieces and roll into sausage shapes. Flour your hands, pinch off pieces of the dough, and add to the soup. Replace the lid and simmer for an additional 5 minutes.

5. Remove the pan from the heat and ladle the soup into warm bowls. Top each with a spoonful of sour cream and serve immediately.

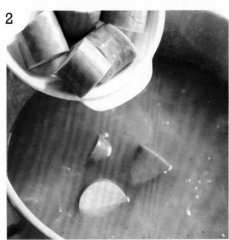

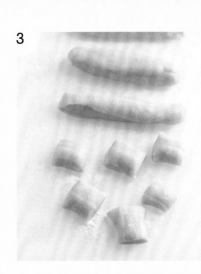

Mixed Bean Soup with Gruyère

 SERVES 4    PREP TIME: 15 minutes    COOKING TIME: 50–55 minutes

nutritional information
per serving   473 cal, 29g fat, 16g sat fat, 9g total sugars, 1.8g salt

Full of beans, vegetables, and fresh herbs and finished with tangy cheese, this is a satisfying soup.

INGREDIENTS

1 tablespoon extra virgin olive oil

3 cloves garlic, finely chopped

4 scallions, sliced, plus extra to serve

3 cups sliced white mushrooms

4 cups vegetable stock

1 large carrot, chopped

2 cups rinsed and drained mixed beans, such as kidney beans, pinto beans, and chickpeas

1 (28-ounce) can diced tomatoes

1 tablespoon chopped fresh thyme

1 tablespoon chopped fresh oregano

1½ cups shredded Gruyère cheese or Swiss cheese

¼ cup heavy cream, plus extra to serve

salt and pepper, to taste

1. Heat the oil in a large saucepan over medium heat. Add the garlic and scallions and cook, stirring, for 3 minutes, until slightly softened. Add the mushrooms and cook, stirring, for an additional 2 minutes.

2. Stir in the stock, then add the carrot, beans, tomatoes, and herbs. Season with salt and pepper. Bring to a boil, then reduce the heat and simmer for 30 minutes.

3. Remove the soup from the heat and let cool slightly. Transfer to a food processor or blender, in batches if necessary, and process until smooth.

4. Return the soup to the rinsed-out pan and stir in the cheese. Cook for an additional 10 minutes, then stir in the cream. Cook for 5 minutes, then remove from the heat. Ladle into warm bowls, top each with a swirl of cream and with scallions. Serve immediately.

1

2

4

HEALTHY HINT

If you are watching calories and fat content, then swap the heavy cream for low-fat Greek yogurt and use just a sprinkling of Gruyère.

Chestnut & Pancetta Soup

SERVES 6 | PREP TIME: 15 minutes | COOKING TIME: 25–30 minutes

nutritional information **per serving** | 335 cal, 16g fat, 4g sat fat, 9g total sugars, 1.4g salt

Chestnuts are the ultimate taste of winter and the delicious combination of smoky pancetta, vegetables, creamy chestnuts, and fresh rosemary makes a filling soup.

INGREDIENTS

3 tablespoons olive oil

6 ounces pancetta, cut into strips

2 onions, finely chopped

2 carrots, finely chopped

2 celery stalks, finely chopped

12 ounces dried chestnuts, soaked overnight, or 30 peeled, fresh or canned whole chestnuts

2 cloves garlic, finely chopped

1 tablespoon finely chopped fresh rosemary

4 cups chicken stock

salt and pepper, to taste

extra virgin olive oil, for drizzling

1. Heat the olive oil in a large saucepan, add the pancetta, and cook over medium heat, stirring frequently, for 2–3 minutes, until starting to brown.

2. Add the onions, carrots, and celery and cook, stirring frequently, for 10 minutes, or until slightly golden and softened.

3. Drain the chestnuts, add to the saucepan with the garlic and rosemary, and stir well. Pour in the stock, bring to a simmer, and cook, uncovered, for 30–35 minutes, until the chestnuts are beginning to soften and break down.

4. Season with salt and pepper. Ladle the soup into warm bowls, drizzle with extra virgin olive oil, and serve immediately.

BE PREPARED
Make up to
two days before
serving, and
keep covered and
chilled in the
refrigerator
until needed.

Beef & Barley Broth

 SERVES 8

 PREP TIME:
15 minutes

 COOKING TIME:
2–2¼ hours

nutritional information per serving	250 cal, 5.5g fat, 2g sat fat, 5g total sugars, 0.2g salt

Traditionally, in an Irish-style broth, the meat is cut up and divided among individual soup bowls before the broth is poured over. A floury potato for mopping up juices tops each bowl.

INGREDIENTS

1½-pound chuck shoulder beef

⅓ cup pearl barley, rinsed

⅓ cup green split peas, rinsed

1 large onion, thickly sliced

½ teaspoon black peppercorns

3 carrots, halved lengthwise and sliced

1 small turnip, diced

1 small leek, green parts included, thinly sliced

1 celery stalk, sliced

8 Yukon gold or white round potatoes

1 cup shredded green cabbage

2 tablespoons chopped fresh parsley

salt, to taste

1. Put the beef, pearl barley, and split peas in a large saucepan with the onion and peppercorns. Pour in enough cold water to just cover. Slowly bring to a boil, skim off any foam from the surface, if necessary, then reduce the heat, cover, and simmer gently for 1½ hours.

2. Add the carrots, turnip, leek, and celery to the pan. Season with salt and simmer for an additional 30 minutes. Add a little more water if the soup starts to look too thick.

3. Meanwhile, put the potatoes in another saucepan with water to cover. Add salt to taste and bring to a boil. Cook for 7–10 minutes, until tender but not disintegrating. Drain, return to the pan, and cover with a clean dish cloth.

4. Remove the meat saucepan from the stove. Carefully lift out the meat, using a slotted spoon. Cut into small cubes and return to the pan. Add the cabbage and simmer for an additional 5 minutes, or until the cabbage is just tender. Season with salt, if needed.

5. Ladle the soup into warm wide soup bowls. Put a potato in the middle of each bowl and sprinkle with the parsley.

Roasted Squash, Garlic & Thyme Soup

 SERVES 6

PREP TIME: 10 minutes

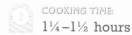 COOKING TIME: 1¼–1½ hours

nutritional information **per serving** | 310 cal, 20g fat, 8g sat fat, 8.5g total sugars, 0.6g salt

Roasting the garlic bulbs brings out the sweetness and adds flavor to this classic soup with a twist.

INGREDIENTS

2 garlic bulbs

¼ cup olive oil, plus extra for drizzling

1 butternut squash or other winter squash (about 2 pounds)

2 tablespoons fresh thyme leaves, plus extra sprigs to garnish

2 tablespoons butter

1 onion, chopped

1 tablespoon all-purpose flour

5 cups chicken stock

½ cup crème fraîche or sour cream

salt and pepper, to taste

1. Preheat the oven to 375°F. Pour ½ tablespoon of the oil over each garlic bulb and season with salt and pepper, then wrap in aluminum foil and put in a large roasting pan. Peel and seed the squash, then cut the flesh into large chunks. Toss the squash in the remaining oil, season with salt and pepper, and sprinkle with half the thyme leaves. Put in the roasting pan in a single layer and cook in the preheated oven for 1 hour.

2. Melt the butter in a large saucepan. Add the onion and cook over medium heat, stirring occasionally, for 5 minutes, until soft. Stir in the flour and cook for 2 minutes. Add the stock, a few spoonfuls at a time to begin with, then add the remainder.

3. When the squash has browned, remove the roasting pan from the oven. Add the squash to the saucepan and simmer for 10 minutes.

4. Open the garlic packages and let cool. When cool enough to handle, break up the garlic bulbs, put the cloves on a cutting board, and press down on each until the garlic pulp squeezes out.

5. Remove the soup from the heat and let cool slightly. Stir in the garlic pulp and the remaining thyme leaves, then transfer to a food processor or blender, in batches if necessary, and process until smooth. Return the soup to the rinsed-out pan and reheat gently; do not boil.

6. Ladle into warm bowls and top each with a spoonful of the crème fraîche or sour cream. Drizzle with a little oil, garnish with thyme sprigs, and serve immediately.

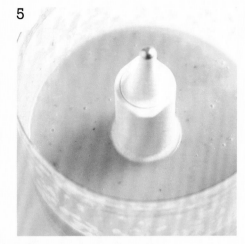

Green Lentil & Vegetable Soup

SERVES 6

PREP TIME:
20 minutes

COOKING TIME:
1–1¼ hours

nutritional information per serving	475 cal, 9g fat, 1.5g sat fat, 6g total sugars, 2.2g salt

Lentils are great in soup because they hold up well during cooking, add texture, and make it more substantial.

INGREDIENTS

3 tablespoons olive oil

1 Spanish onion, chopped

3 cloves garlic, chopped

2 celery stalks, chopped

1 carrot, chopped

1 potato, chopped

6 ounces smoked ham, chopped

2¼ cups green or brown lentils

12½ cups vegetable stock

1 bay leaf

4 fresh parsley sprigs

4 tomatoes, peeled and chopped

1½ teaspoons sweet paprika

¼ cup sherry vinegar

salt and pepper, to taste

1. Heat the oil in a large saucepan. Add the onion, garlic, celery, carrot, and potato and cook over low heat, stirring occasionally, for 5–7 minutes, until softened. Add the ham and cook, stirring occasionally, for an additional 3 minutes. Remove from the pan with a slotted spoon and set aside.

2. Add the lentils, stock, bay leaf, and parsley sprigs to the pan, increase the heat to medium, and bring to a boil. Reduce the heat and simmer, stirring occasionally, for 30 minutes.

3. Add the tomatoes and return the ham to the pan. Stir well and simmer for an additional 25–30 minutes.

4. Remove and discard the bay leaf and parsley. Stir in the paprika and vinegar, season with salt and pepper, and heat through for 2–3 minutes. Ladle into warm soup bowls and serve immediately.

1

2

3

Carrot & Coriander Soup

 SERVES 6

 PREP TIME:
15 minutes

 COOKING TIME:
35–40 minutes

nutritional information per serving	205 cal, 10g fat, 3g sat fat, 9g total sugars, 0.6g salt

This version of the classic soup is made extra special and is packed with flavor by the addition of toasted coriander seeds and plenty of fresh cilantro.

INGREDIENTS

3 tablespoons olive oil

1 red onion, chopped

1 large potato, chopped

1 celery stalk, chopped

8 carrots, chopped

4 cups vegetable stock

1 tablespoon butter

2 teaspoons coriander seeds, crushed

1½ tablespoons chopped fresh cilantro, plus extra to garnish

1 cup milk

salt and pepper, to taste

1. Heat the oil in a large saucepan. Add the onion and cook over low heat, stirring occasionally, for 5 minutes, until softened.

2. Add the potato and celery and cook, stirring occasionally, for 5 minutes, then add the carrots and cook for an additional 5 minutes. Cover the pan, reduce the heat to low, and cook, shaking the pan occasionally, for 10 minutes.

3. Pour in the stock and bring to a boil, then cover and simmer for 10 minutes, until the vegetables are tender.

4. Meanwhile, melt the butter in a skillet. Add the coriander seeds and cook, stirring continuously, for 1 minute. Add the chopped cilantro and cook, stirring continuously, for 1 minute, then remove from the heat.

5. Remove the soup from the heat and let cool slightly. Transfer to a food processor or blender, in batches if necessary, and process until smooth. Return the soup to the rinsed-out pan, stir in the coriander mixture and milk and season with salt and pepper. Reheat gently, then serve, sprinkled with chopped cilantro.

Split Pea & Ham Soup

 SERVES 8

 PREP TIME:
10 minutes

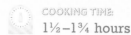 COOKING TIME:
1½–1¾ hours

nutritional information
per serving · 294 cal, 4.5g fat, 1g sat fat, 3.5g total sugars, 1.2g salt

Although this isn't quick to cook, it is worth waiting for the fresh herbs to release their flavor while cooking.

INGREDIENTS

2½ cups split green peas

1 tablespoon olive oil

1 large onion, finely chopped

1 large carrot, finely chopped

1 celery stalk, finely chopped

4 cups chicken stock
or vegetable stock

4 cups water

8 ounces lean smoked ham,
finely diced

¼ teaspoon dried thyme

¼ teaspoon dried marjoram

1 bay leaf

salt and pepper, to taste

1. Rinse the peas under cold running water. Put them in a saucepan and cover with water. Bring to a boil and boil for 3 minutes, skimming any foam from the surface, if necessary. Drain the peas.

2. Heat the oil in a large saucepan over medium heat. Add the onion and cook for 3–4 minutes, stirring occasionally, until just softened. Add the carrot and celery and continue cooking for 2 minutes.

3. Add the peas, pour in the stock and water, and stir to combine.

4. Bring just to a boil and stir the ham into the soup. Add the thyme, marjoram, and bay leaf. Reduce the heat, cover, and cook gently for 1–1½ hours, until the ingredients are soft. Remove the bay leaf.

5. Season with salt and pepper, if necessary, then ladle into warm soup bowls and serve.

GOES WELL WITH
Try making soda
bread (page 310)
and serve warm
with the soup.

Barley, Lentil & Onion Soup

 SERVES 6    PREP TIME: 20 minutes plus drying    COOKING TIME: 2–2¼ hours

nutritional information per serving	271 cal, 10g fat, 1.5g sat fat, 6.5g total sugars, 0.8g salt

Ginger, cumin, and lemon are perfect for wintry days, when you need a lift and a nutritious boost.

INGREDIENTS

2 tablespoons pearl barley

⅔ cup water

7 cups vegetable stock

3 onions, thinly sliced into rings

¾ cup green lentils

½ teaspoon ground ginger

1 teaspoon ground cumin

3 tablespoons lemon juice

2 tablespoons chopped fresh cilantro

salt and pepper, to taste

to garnish

2 onions, halved and thinly sliced

⅓ cup vegetable oil

2 cloves garlic, finely chopped

1. Put the barley into a large saucepan, pour in the water, and bring to a boil. Reduce the heat, cover, and simmer gently, stirring frequently, for about 30 minutes, until all the liquid has been absorbed.

2. Add the stock, onions, lentils, ginger, and cumin and bring to a boil over medium heat. Reduce the heat, cover, and simmer, stirring occasionally, for 1½ hours, adding a little more stock, if necessary.

3. Meanwhile, make the garnish. Spread out the onions on a layer of paper towels and cover with another layer. Let dry out for 30 minutes. Heat the oil in a skillet. Add the onions and cook over low heat, stirring continuously, for about 20 minutes, until well browned. Add the garlic and cook, stirring continuously, for an additional 5 minutes. Remove the onions with a slotted spoon and drain well on paper towels.

4. Season the soup with salt and pepper, stir in the lemon juice and cilantro, and simmer for an additional 5 minutes. Serve garnished with the browned onions.

Broccoli & Stilton Soup

 SERVES 4   PREP TIME: 15 minutes   COOKING TIME: 35 minutes

nutritional information per serving | 451 cal, 23g fat, 14g sat fat, 6.5g total sugars, 2g salt

This often ignored vegetable is given a tasty twist with creamy mild Stilton in this classic soup.

INGREDIENTS

3 tablespoons butter

2 onions, chopped

1 large potato, chopped

1 head of broccoli, cut into florets

6 cups vegetable stock

6 ounces Stilton cheese or other blue cheese, diced

pinch of ground mace

salt and pepper, to taste

croutons, to garnish

1. Melt the butter in a large saucepan. Add the onions and potato and stir well. Cover and cook over low heat for 7 minutes. Add the broccoli and stir well, then replace the lid and cook for an additional 5 minutes.

2. Increase the heat to medium, pour in the stock, and bring to a boil. Reduce the heat, season with salt and pepper, and replace the lid. Simmer for 15–20 minutes, until the vegetables are tender.

3. Remove the pan from the heat, strain into a bowl, reserving the vegetables, and let cool slightly. Transfer the vegetables to a food processor or blender, add one ladleful of the stock, and process until smooth. Gradually add the remaining stock.

4. Return the soup to the rinsed-out pan and reheat gently. Remove from the heat and stir in the cheese until melted and thoroughly combined. Stir in the mace and season to taste, if necessary. Ladle into bowls, sprinkle with the croutons, and serve.

1

3

4

GOES WELL WITH
Instead of making regular croutons, try lightly toasting some small, thin slices of ciabatta or baguette and float on top of the soup.

Vegetable & Corn Chowder

 SERVES 4    PREP TIME: 10 minutes    COOKING TIME: 35–40 minutes

nutritional information per serving	400 cal, 16g fat, 8g sat fat, 16g total sugars, 1.2g salt

Although traditionally made with seafood, this milk-based soup is simple yet delicious and satisfying to eat.

INGREDIENTS

1 tablespoon vegetable oil

1 red onion, diced

1 red bell pepper, seeded and diced

3 cloves garlic, crushed

3 Yukon gold, red-skinned, or white round potatoes, diced

2 tablespoons all-purpose flour

2½ cups milk

1¼ cups vegetable stock

¾ cup broccoli florets

1 (11-ounce) can corn kernels, drained

⅔ cup shredded cheddar cheese

salt and pepper, to taste

1. Heat the oil in a large saucepan. Add the onion, red bell pepper, garlic, and potatoes and sauté over low heat, stirring frequently, for 2–3 minutes.

2. Stir in the flour and cook, stirring, for 30 seconds. Gradually stir in the milk and stock.

3. Add the broccoli and corn. Bring the mixture to a boil, stirring continuously, then reduce the heat and simmer for about 20 minutes, or until all the vegetables are tender.

4. Stir in half of the cheese until it melts. Season with salt and pepper and ladle into warm bowls. Garnish with the remaining cheese and serve immediately.

Cheese & Bacon Soup

 SERVES 4

 PREP TIME:
15 minutes

 COOKING TIME:
45–50 minutes

nutritional information **per serving**	793 cal, 62g fat, 31g sat fat, 4.5g total sugars, 5.2g salt

A hearty soup is an ideal end to a dark winter's day. Smoky bacon, leeks, potatoes, and cheese meld together in perfect harmony.

INGREDIENTS

2 tablespoons butter

2 cloves garlic, finely chopped

1 large onion, thinly sliced

8 ounces smoked lean bacon, chopped

2 large leeks, trimmed and thinly sliced

2 tablespoons all-purpose flour

4 cups vegetable stock

4 Yukon gold or white round potatoes, chopped

½ cup heavy cream

2½ cups shredded cheddar cheese, plus extra to garnish

salt and pepper, to taste

1. Melt the butter in a large saucepan over medium heat. Add the garlic and onion and cook, stirring, for 3 minutes, until slightly softened. Add the chopped bacon and leeks and cook for an additional 3 minutes, stirring.

2. In a bowl, mix the flour with enough stock to make a smooth paste, then stir it into the pan. Cook, stirring, for 2 minutes. Pour in the remaining stock, then add the potatoes. Season with salt and pepper. Bring the soup to a boil, then lower the heat and simmer gently for 25 minutes, until the potatoes are tender and cooked through.

3. Stir in the cream and cook for 5 minutes, then gradually stir in the cheese until melted. Ladle into warm bowls. Garnish with shredded cheddar cheese and serve immediately.

1

2

3

GOES WELL WITH
A light accompaniment is needed for such a creamy soup—try toasted pita bread or Italian-style bread sticks.

Chicken Noodle Soup

 SERVES 6

 PREP TIME:
5 minutes

 COOKING TIME:
30–35 minutes

nutritional information per serving	170 cal, 2g fat, 0.5g sat fat, 4g total sugars, 0.7g salt

For many, this is the ultimate cure for winter ailments—it's packed with nutritious ingredients and quickly warms you up.

INGREDIENTS

2 skinless, boneless chicken breasts

5 cups water or chicken stock

3 carrots, peeled and cut into ¼-inch slices

4 ounces egg noodles

salt and pepper, to taste

fresh tarragon leaves, to garnish

1. Put the chicken breasts in a large saucepan over medium heat, add the water, and bring to a simmer. Cook for 25–30 minutes. Skim any foam from the surface, if necessary. Remove the chicken from the stock and keep warm.

2. Continue to simmer the stock, add the carrots and noodles, and cook for 4–5 minutes.

3. Thinly slice or shred the chicken breasts and put in warm serving bowls.

4. Season the soup with salt and pepper and pour it over the chicken. Serve at once, garnished with the tarragon.

COOK'S NOTE
Clean hands are the fastest tools for shredding cooked chicken, flaking cooked fish, crumbling cheese, and tearing delicate salad greens and herbs.

Butternut Squash
& Smoky Bacon Soup

 SERVES 4    PREP TIME:
20 minutes    COOKING TIME:
45–50 minutes

nutritional information
per serving   254 cal, 13g fat, 3.5g sat fat, 11g total sugars, 1.5g salt

Here is a silky smooth soup packed with flavor and garnished with crispy bacon and toasted seeds.

INGREDIENTS

2 tablespoons olive oil

5 bacon strips, chopped

1 large onion, coarsely chopped

2 celery stalks, coarsely chopped

2 teaspoons chopped fresh
thyme leaves

1 butternut squash, peeled,
seeded, and cut into chunks

1 large red bell pepper, seeded
and coarsely chopped

2½ cups vegetable stock

½ teaspoon smoked paprika

crispy cooked bacon and toasted
pumpkin seeds, to garnish

1. Heat the oil in a large saucepan over low heat. Add the bacon and cook until the fat from the bacon starts to run. Stir in the onion, celery, and thyme. Cover and cook for 10 minutes, until softened.

2. Stir in the squash, red bell pepper, stock, and smoked paprika. Bring to a boil, then reduce the heat, cover, and simmer for 30 minutes, until the vegetables are tender. Remove from the heat and let cool slightly.

3. Transfer the soup to a food processor or blender, in batches if necessary, and process until smooth. Return to the rinsed-out pan and heat through. Ladle into warm bowls or mugs, garnish with crispy cooked bacon and toasted pumpkin seeds, and serve immediately.

COOK'S NOTE
The skin of butternut squash breaks down easily in cooking, so simply roast with the skin intact to save time.

Roasted Sweet Potato & Garlic Soup

 SERVES 6  PREP TIME: 5 minutes 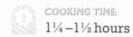 COOKING TIME: 1¼–1½ hours

nutritional information per serving	226 cal, 11g fat, 5g sat fat, 9g total sugars, 0.5g salt

This soup has an appetizing combination of color and taste—roasting the root vegetables intensifies their sweet, earthy flavors.

INGREDIENTS

1 acorn or butternut squash
2 large sweet potatoes
4 shallots
2 tablespoons olive oil
6 cloves garlic, unpeeled
3½ cups chicken stock
½ cup crème fraîche or Greek yogurt
salt and pepper, to taste
snipped fresh chives, to garnish

1. Preheat the oven to 375°F. Cut the squash, sweet potato, and shallots in half lengthwise, all the way to the stem end. Scoop the seeds out of the squash. Brush a shallow roasting pan with the oil.

2. Put the vegetables, cut side down, in the prepared pan and add the garlic. Roast in the preheated oven for about 40 minutes, until tender and light brown. Set aside and let cool.

3. When cool, scoop the flesh from the sweet potato and squash halves and put in a saucepan. Peel the shallots and garlic and add to the other vegetables.

4. Add the stock. Bring just to a boil, reduce the heat, and simmer, partly covered, for about 30 minutes, stirring occasionally, until the vegetables are tender.

5. Let the soup cool slightly, then transfer to a food processor and process, in batches if necessary, until smooth.

6. Return the soup to the rinsed-out saucepan. Season with salt and pepper, then simmer for 5–10 minutes, until heated through. Stir in the crème fraîche or yogurt, then ladle into serving bowls, garnish with snipped chives, and serve.

Healthy Soups

Lentil & Spinach Soup

 SERVES 4

 PREP TIME:
10 minutes

 COOKING TIME:
40–45 minutes

nutritional information
per serving

270 cal, 2.5g fat, 0.5g sat fat, 8g total sugars, 0.9g salt

A wonderful fresh and fragrant soup—light yet packed with flavor and nutrients, this soup is simple to make and great to eat at any time of the day.

INGREDIENTS

1 teaspoon vegetable oil

1 onion, finely chopped

2 cloves garlic, finely chopped

2 celery stalks, trimmed and finely chopped

3 carrots, peeled and finely chopped

½ teaspoon chili powder

1 teaspoon smoked paprika

1 teaspoon whole cumin seeds

1 cup dried red lentils, washed

4 cups vegetable stock

1 cup coarsely chopped spinach, thawed if frozen

6 cherry tomatoes, halved

¼ cup plain yogurt, to serve

salt and pepper, to serve

1. Heat the oil in a large saucepan over medium heat. Add the onion, garlic, celery, and carrots, and cook for 4–5 minutes, or until starting to soften.

2. Add the chili powder, paprika, and cumin seeds and cook for an additional 1 minute, stirring continuously.

3. Add the lentils and stock, season with salt and pepper, bring to a boil, and cook for 10 minutes. Cover and reduce the heat, then simmer for 20–25 minutes, until the vegetables and lentils are cooked.

4. Add the spinach and tomatoes and cook for 5 minutes, or until the spinach has wilted. Season with salt and pepper, if necessary. Serve immediately with a tablespoon of yogurt in each bowl.

Lantern Soup

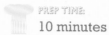

nutritional information per serving	130 cal, 1.5g fat, 0.5g sat fat, 4g total sugars, 1.3g salt

This hearty soup is guaranteed to keep you fuller for longer and is packed with flavor and goodness.

INGREDIENTS

1 teaspoon olive oil

1 red onion, chopped

2 cloves garlic, crushed

4 cups peeled, seeded, and chopped pumpkin or other winter squash

2 teaspoons smoked paprika

¼ teaspoon crushed red pepper flakes

5–6 fresh sage leaves, finely chopped

3¾ cups vegetable stock

1 (15-ounce) can navy beans, drained

salt and pepper, to taste

handful fresh flat-leaf parsley, finely chopped

1. Heat the oil in a saucepan and sauté the onion and garlic for 3–4 minutes. Add the pumpkin and cook for an additional 4–5 minutes.

2. Add the paprika, red pepper flakes, and sage and cook for 1 minute, stirring all the time.

3. Add the stock, season with salt and pepper, cover, and simmer for 20–25 minutes, or until the pumpkin is tender. Let the soup cool slightly, then process using a handheld immersion blender, until smooth.

4. Stir in the navy beans and heat through for 2–3 minutes. Serve garnished with a little of the parsley.

1

3

4

FREEZING TIP

Let cool completely at the end of step 3, then transfer to an airtight container and freeze for up to three months. Defrost and warm through, then stir in the beans and complete as directed.

Carrot, Celery & Apple Soup

 SERVES 4    PREP TIME: 15 minutes    COOKING TIME: 35–40 minutes

nutritional information per serving	174 cal, 3g fat, 1g sat fat, 31g total sugars, 0.5g salt

A wonderful light soup, perfect for days when you want to watch your fat intake without compromising on taste.

INGREDIENTS

15 carrots (about 2 pounds), finely diced

1 onion, chopped

3 celery stalks, diced

4 cups low-sodium vegetable stock

2 Pippin or Gala apples

2 tablespoons tomato paste

1 bay leaf

salt and pepper, to taste

to garnish

1 medium Pippin or Gala apple, thinly sliced

juice of ½ lemon

shredded celery leaves

1. Put the carrots, onion, and celery in a large saucepan and add the stock. Bring to a boil, reduce the heat, cover, and simmer for 10 minutes.

2. Meanwhile, peel, core, and dice the apples. Add the diced apple, tomato paste, and bay leaf to the saucepan and bring to a boil over medium heat. Reduce the heat, cover, and simmer for 20 minutes. Remove and discard the bay leaf.

3. Meanwhile, to make the garnish, put the apple slices in a small saucepan and pour the lemon juice over the slices. Heat the apple slices gently and simmer for 1–2 minutes, or until the apple is tender. Drain the apple slices and reserve until required.

4. Transfer the carrot-and-apple mixture to a food processor or blender, in batches if necessary, and process until smooth. Return the soup to the rinsed-out saucepan, reheat gently, and season with salt and pepper. Ladle the soup into warm bowls, top with the reserved apple slices and shredded celery leaves, and serve immediately.

Consommé

 SERVES 6

 PREP TIME:
15 minutes

 COOKING TIME:
1¼–1½ hours

nutritional information per serving	150 cal, 4g fat, 1.5g sat fat, 9g total sugars, 0.7g salt

This clarified broth is a classic dish, versions of which have been served over the course of many centuries. This recipe follows the tradition of using egg whites to draw the impurities to the surface.

INGREDIENTS

5¼ cups strong beef stock

8 ounces fresh ground round or ground sirloin beef

2 tomatoes, skinned, seeded, and chopped

2 large carrots, chopped

1 large onion, chopped

2 celery stalks, chopped

1 turnip, chopped (optional)

1 bouquet garni (sprigs of parsley, bay leaf, and thyme tied together)

2–3 egg whites

shells of 2–4 eggs, crushed

1–2 tablespoons sherry (optional)

salt and pepper, to taste

julienne strips of raw carrot, turnip, celery, or celeriac, to garnish

1. Put the stock and beef in a saucepan and let sit for 1 hour. Add the tomatoes, carrots, onion, celery, turnip (if using), bouquet garni, two of the egg whites, the crushed shells of two of the eggs, and plenty of salt and pepper. Bring almost to boiling point, whisking hard all the time.

2. Cover and simmer for 1 hour, being careful not to let the layer of froth on top of the soup break.

3. Pour the soup through a jelly bag or scalded fine cheesecloth into a large heatproof bowl, then repeat, pouring the mixture into a clean pan. The resulting liquid should be clear.

4. If the soup is not clear, return it to the pan with another egg white and the crushed shells of two more eggs. Repeat the whisking process as before and then boil for 10 minutes. Strain again.

5. Add the sherry, if using, to the soup and reheat gently; do not boil. Put the garnish in warm bowls and carefully pour in the broth. Serve immediately.

Roasted Mediterranean Vegetable Soup

 SERVES 6

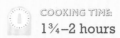 PREP TIME: 5 minutes

COOKING TIME: 1¾–2 hours

nutritional information per serving	173 cal, 8g fat, 1.5g sat fat, 8g total sugars, 0.7g salt

A real taste of the Mediterranean, with plenty of flavor and little in the way of fat and calories.

INGREDIENTS

2 eggplants

4 tomatoes

2 red bell peppers

2 onions, unpeeled

2 cloves garlic, unpeeled

¼ cup olive oil

1 fresh oregano sprig

6 cups chicken stock or vegetable stock

salt and pepper, to taste

chopped fresh basil, to garnish

1. Preheat the oven to 350°F. Prick the eggplants several times with a fork and put in a roasting pan. Add the tomatoes, bell peppers, and unpeeled onions and garlic. Sprinkle with 2 tablespoons of the oil. Roast in the preheated oven for 30 minutes, then remove the tomatoes. Roast the eggplants, peppers, onions, and garlic for an additional 30 minutes, until soft and the pepper skins have blackened.

2. Put the cooked roasted vegetables in a bowl, cover with a damp dish towel, and let sit for 3–4 hours or overnight, until cold. When cold, cut the eggplants in half, scoop out the flesh, and put in the bowl. Remove the skin from the tomatoes, cut in half and discard the seeds, and add the flesh to the bowl. Hold the bell peppers over the bowl to collect the juices and peel off the skin. Remove the stem, core, and seeds and add the flesh to the bowl. Peel the onions, cut into quarters, and add to the bowl. Squeeze the garlic cloves out of their skin into the bowl.

3. Heat the remaining oil in a large saucepan. Add the vegetables and their juices and the leaves from the oregano sprig, season with salt and pepper, then cook gently, stirring frequently, for 30 minutes. Add the stock and bring to a boil, then simmer for 30 minutes.

4. Remove the saucepan from the heat and let cool slightly. Transfer to a food processor or blender, in batches if necessary, and process until smooth. Return the soup to the rinsed-out pan and reheat gently; do not boil. Ladle into warm bowls, garnish with basil, and serve immediately.

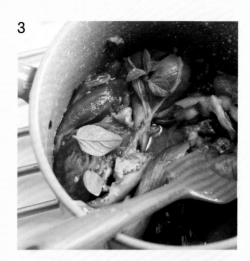

Paprika-Spiced Vegetable Soup

 SERVES 6    PREP TIME: 15 minutes    COOKING TIME: 1¼–1½ hours

nutritional information per serving	181 cal, 4.5g fat, 0.7g sat fat, 9.5g total sugars, 0.5g salt

Hungarian in origin and traditionally made with beef, this vegetarian version is hearty and full of flavor.

INGREDIENTS

2 tablespoons olive oil

1 large onion, chopped

2 cloves garlic, finely chopped

3–4 carrots, thinly sliced

½ head of savoy cabbage, cored and shredded

1 small red bell pepper, seeded and chopped

1 tablespoon all-purpose flour

2 tablespoons sweet paprika

4 cups vegetable stock

2 Yukon gold or white round potatoes, cut into chunks

1–2 teaspoons sugar (optional)

salt and pepper, to taste

crème fraîche or Greek yogurt, to garnish

1. Heat the oil in a large saucepan. Add the onion, garlic, and carrots and cook over low heat, stirring occasionally, for 8–10 minutes, until lightly browned.

2. Add the cabbage and red bell pepper and cook, stirring frequently, for 3–4 minutes. Sprinkle in the flour and paprika and cook, stirring continuously, for 1 minute. Gradually stir in the stock, a little at a time. Increase the heat to medium and bring to a boil, stirring continuously.

3. Season with salt, reduce the heat, cover, and simmer for 30 minutes. Add the potatoes and bring back to a boil, then reduce the heat, re-place the lid, and simmer for an additional 20–30 minutes, until the potatoes are soft but not falling apart.

4. Season with salt and pepper, if necessary, and add the sugar, if using. Ladle the soup into warm bowls, swirl a little crème fraîche or yogurt on top of each, and serve immediately.

1

2

3

Carrot & Parsnip Soup

 SERVES 6  PREP TIME: 10 minutes  COOKING TIME: 30–35 minutes

nutritional information **per serving**	92 cal, 1g fat, 0.2g sat fat, 8g total sugars, 0.4g salt

Carrots and parsnips are both naturally sweet, and they work together well in soup. The chervil's flavor adds a delicious freshness to this light and simple recipe.

INGREDIENTS

6 carrots, chopped
3 parsnips, chopped
4 shallots, chopped
4 fresh chervil sprigs
3½ cups vegetable stock
salt and pepper, to taste
heavy cream, to garnish

1. Put the carrots, parsnips, shallots, and chervil into a saucepan, pour in the stock, and season with salt and pepper. Bring to a boil, reduce the heat, and simmer for 20–25 minutes, until the vegetables are tender.

2. Remove the pan from the heat and let cool slightly. Remove and discard the chervil, then transfer to a food processor or blender, in batches if necessary, and process until smooth.

3. Return the soup to the rinsed-out pan and reheat gently; do not boil. Ladle into warm bowls, swirl about 1 tablespoon of cream on the top of each, and serve.

1

2
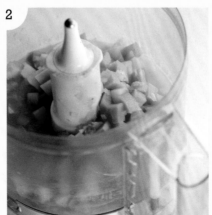

3
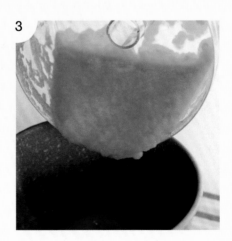

COOK'S NOTE
If you prefer, don't peel the carrots and parsnips—a quick scrub will be enough.

Chicken & Lentil Soup

 SERVES 6

 PREP TIME:
15 minutes

 COOKING TIME:
1¼–1½ hours

nutritional information per serving	310 cal, 8.5g fat, 1.5g sat fat, 5g total sugars, 0.7g salt

The lentils add a delicious nutty texture and flavor to this soup, and help to keep you fuller for longer.

INGREDIENTS

3 tablespoons olive oil

1 large onion, chopped

2 leeks, chopped

2 carrots, chopped

2 celery stalks, chopped

3 cups chopped white button mushrooms

¼ cup dry white wine

5 cups vegetable stock

1 bay leaf

2 teaspoons dried mixed herbs

1 cup dried green lentils

2½ cups diced, cooked boneless chicken

salt and pepper, to taste

1. Heat the oil in a large saucepan. Add the onion, leeks, carrots, celery, and mushrooms and cook over low heat, stirring occasionally, for 5–7 minutes, until softened but not browned.

2. Increase the heat to medium, pour in the wine, and cook for 2–3 minutes, until the alcohol has evaporated, then pour in the stock.

3. Bring to a boil, add the bay leaf and herbs, reduce the heat, cover, and simmer for 30 minutes. Add the lentils, replace the lid, and simmer, stirring occasionally, for an additional 40 minutes, until they are tender.

4. Stir in the chicken, season with salt and pepper, and simmer for an additional 5–10 minutes, until heated through. Serve immediately.

Thai-Spiced Sweet Potato Soup

 SERVES 6

 PREP TIME:
10 minutes

 COOKING TIME:
30 minutes

nutritional information per serving	334 cal, 13g fat, 9.5g sat fat, 12g total sugars, 1g salt

A gorgeous vibrant soup with a real kick from both the Thai spices and fresh ginger. The coconut milk adds flavor as well as a creamy texture to the soup.

INGREDIENTS

2 teaspoons vegetable oil

1 onion, diced

1 tablespoon finely chopped fresh ginger

1 tablespoon Thai red curry paste

4 sweet potatoes, peeled and diced

1¾ cups coconut milk

4 cups vegetable stock

juice of 1 lime

1 cup finely chopped fresh cilantro, to garnish

1. In a large, heavy saucepan, heat the oil over medium–high heat. Add the onion and ginger and cook, stirring, for about 5 minutes, or until soft.

2. Add the curry paste and cook, stirring, for an additional minute or so. Add the sweet potatoes, coconut milk, and vegetable stock and bring to a boil. Reduce the heat to medium and simmer, uncovered, for about 20 minutes, or until the sweet potatoes are soft.

3. Process using a handheld immersion blender, until smooth. Return the soup to the heat and bring back up to a simmer. Just before serving, stir in the lime juice. Serve hot, garnished with cilantro.

Roasted Tomato Soup

 SERVES 4  PREP TIME: 25 minutes  COOKING TIME: 1¼ hours

nutritional information per serving	305 cal, 15g fat, 2.5g sat fat, 12g total sugars, 1.2g salt

This fuss-free recipe is perfect if you're busy in the kitchen, because all the hard work is done for you in the oven, and there are no pans to watch over.

INGREDIENTS

20 plum tomatoes
(about 3 pounds), halved,
stem ends removed

1 red onion, coarsely chopped

6 cloves garlic, peeled

2 tablespoons olive oil

1 teaspoon pepper

6 sprigs fresh thyme

4 cups vegetable stock

2 tablespoons lemon juice

salt, to taste

parmesan croutons

3½ slices whole-wheat bread,
cut in cubes

2 tablespoons olive oil

¼ teaspoon pepper

2 tablespoons grated
Parmesan cheese

1. Preheat the oven to 450°F. Put the tomatoes, onion, and garlic on a large baking sheet with the olive oil, pepper, and thyme, season with salt, and toss together. Spread the vegetables out into a single layer, arranging the tomatoes cut side up, and roast in the preheated oven for about 45 minutes, or until the vegetables are soft.

2. To make the croutons, reduce the oven heat to 300°F. Toss the cubed bread in the olive oil, sprinkle with the pepper, and season with salt. Spread the bread cubes in an even layer on a baking sheet and bake in the preheated oven for about 25 minutes. Sprinkle with the cheese, return to the oven, and bake for an additional 5 minutes, or until the cheese is melted and beginning to brown.

3. Finish the soup while the croutons are baking. Put the roasted vegetables and stock in a large saucepan and process, using a handheld immersion blender, until smooth.

4. Bring the soup to a boil, reduce the heat, and simmer, stirring occasionally, for about 15 minutes. Just before serving, stir in the lemon juice. Serve hot, garnished with croutons.

1

2

3

Chicken & Thyme Soup

 SERVES 6    PREP TIME: 10 minutes    COOKING TIME: 30–35 minutes

nutritional information per serving	300 cal, 3.5g fat, 0.5g sat fat, 4g total sugars, 0.8g salt

This big broth, packed with vegetables, herbs, and pasta, as well as a hint of lemon, is super healthy. It's great for feeding a hungry family, or make a batch and lunch will be taken care of for a few days.

INGREDIENTS

1 tablespoon olive oil

1 onion, diced

4 cloves garlic, finely chopped

2 carrots, diced

2 celery stalks, diced

6 cups chicken stock

4 sprigs fresh thyme

1 bay leaf

½ teaspoon pepper, plus extra to garnish

1 pound skinless, boneless chicken breasts

8 ounces dried pasta

grated zest and juice of 1 lemon

1. In a large, heavy saucepan, heat the oil over medium–high heat. Add the onion and garlic and sauté, stirring frequently, for about 5 minutes, or until soft. Add the carrots and celery and cook for an additional 1–2 minutes. Add the stock, thyme, bay leaf, and pepper and bring to a boil.

2. Reduce heat to medium–low and add the chicken breasts. Simmer for about 20 minutes, or until the chicken is cooked through without any signs of pink when the thickest part of the meat is cut through with a sharp knife. Remove the chicken from the pan and set aside. When cool enough to handle, cut the chicken into bite-size pieces.

3. Remove the thyme sprigs and bay leaf from the soup and discard them. Return the soup to a simmer over medium heat.

4. Cook the pasta according to package directions and drain. Add the cooked pasta and cooked chicken to the soup and simmer for about 5 minutes, or until heated through. Just before serving, stir in the lemon zest and juice. Serve immediately, garnished with pepper.

Spicy Corn Chowder

 SERVES 6

 PREP TIME:
15 minutes

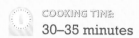 COOKING TIME:
30–35 minutes

nutritional information **per serving**   188 cal, 5.5g fat, 0.8g sat fat, 6.5g total sugars, 0.5g salt

An unusual twist on a classic chowder, in this recipe silken tofu is pureed to add a creamy texture, which complements the vegetables and fresh herbs.

INGREDIENTS

1 tablespoon olive oil

1 onion, diced

2 cloves garlic, finely chopped

2 carrots, diced

2 celery stalks, diced

1 red bell pepper, seeded and diced

3 cups frozen corn kernels

½ teaspoon chili powder

4 cups vegetable stock

8 ounces silken tofu, drained

2 tablespoons chopped cilantro, to garnish

3 scallions, thinly sliced, to garnish

1. Heat the oil in a large skillet over medium–high heat. Add the onion and garlic and cook, stirring occasionally, for about 5 minutes, or until soft.

2. Add the carrots, celery, bell pepper, corn, chili powder, and stock. Bring to a boil, reduce the heat to medium–low, and simmer, uncovered, for about 20 minutes, or until the vegetables are soft.

3. Process the tofu along with a ladleful of the soup in a blender or food processor until smooth. Stir the tofu mixture into the soup and simmer for 5 minutes, or until heated through. Serve hot, garnished with the cilantro and scallions.

Roasted Root Vegetable Soup with Ginger

 SERVES 6

 PREP TIME:
10 minutes

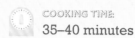 COOKING TIME:
35–40 minutes

nutritional information per serving	210 cal, 13g fat, 2g sat fat, 8g total sugars, 0.5g salt

This is a big soup full of flavor and goodness and a great hit of heat from the garnish of sautéed ginger shreds. If you're feeling a little under the weather or needing a lift, this is the perfect remedy.

INGREDIENTS

1 onion

1 sweet potato

½ small rutabaga (or an extra ½ sweet potato)

2 carrots

1 potato

⅓ cup olive oil

2 tablespoons tomato paste

¼ teaspoon pepper

2 cloves garlic, peeled

2 tablespoons peanut oil

2 (2-inch) pieces fresh ginger, thinly sliced

3½ cups vegetable stock

½ teaspoon sea salt

crème fraîche or Greek yogurt, to serve

coarsely chopped fresh flat-leaf parsley, to garnish

1. Preheat the oven to 375°F. Peel the vegetables and cut into large, even chunks.

2. Mix the olive oil, tomato paste, and pepper in a large bowl. Add the vegetables and the garlic and toss to coat.

3. Spread out the vegetables in a roasting pan. Roast in the preheated oven for 20 minutes, or until the garlic is soft. Remove the garlic and set aside. Roast the vegetables for an additional 10–15 minutes, until tender.

4. Meanwhile, heat the peanut oil in a skillet over high heat. Add the ginger and sauté, turning continuously, for 1–2 minutes, until crisp. Immediately remove the ginger from the skillet and drain on paper towels. Set aside and keep warm.

5. Transfer the garlic and the other roasted vegetables to a food processor or blender. Process in short bursts to a coarse paste.

6. Pour the paste into a saucepan and add the stock. Add the salt, then simmer, stirring, for 1–2 minutes, until heated through. Ladle the soup into warm serving bowls and swirl in a little crème fraîche or yogurt. Sprinkle with parsley and serve.

Sweet Potato & Green Bean Soup

 SERVES 4 PREP TIME: 10 minutes COOKING TIME: 50–55 minutes

nutritional information per serving	190 cal, 2g fat, 0.7g sat fat, 12g total sugars, 0.9g salt

Generously seasoned with garlic, this is certainly not for those who avoid bold flavors.

INGREDIENTS

1 bulb garlic
2 teaspoons olive oil
1 onion, chopped
2 cups chopped sweet potatoes
4 cups vegetable stock
1 cup finely chopped green beans
1¼ cup low-fat plain yogurt
salt and pepper, to taste
1 tablespoon snipped fresh chives, to garnish

1. Preheat the oven to 375°F. Pull the garlic bulb apart and put in a small roasting pan. Roast in the preheated oven for 20 minutes, or until soft. Remove and let cool before squeezing out the soft insides. Reserve.

2. Heat the oil in a heavy saucepan over medium heat, add the onion and sweet potatoes, and cook, stirring continuously, for 5 minutes. Add the stock and bring to a boil. Cover with a lid, reduce the heat, and simmer for 10 minutes. Add the green beans and the roasted garlic and continue to simmer for 10 minutes, or until the potatoes are tender. Remove and let cool slightly.

3. Reserve 2 tablespoons of the cooked green beans, then transfer the remaining beans to a food processor or blender, in batches if necessary, and process until smooth. Return the soup to the rinsed-out saucepan, add the reserved beans, and season with salt and pepper.

4. Ladle the soup into warm bowls, swirl a spoonful of yogurt in each, and garnish with snipped chives. Serve immediately.

1

2

3

COOK'S NOTE
Roasting whole garlic cloves is a great way of mellowing the harshness of garlic. It sweetens it and transforms it into a delicious purée.

Curried Lentil Soup

 SERVES 2    PREP TIME: 15 minutes    COOKING TIME: 50–55 minutes

nutritional information **per serving**	176 cal, 3g fat, 0.5g sat fat, 10g total sugars, 0.7g salt

Lightly spiced lentil soup can be adjusted to your taste—simply add more or less curry paste, and add a little chopped chile if you prefer hot food.

INGREDIENTS

1 teaspoon vegetable oil

1 teaspoon mild curry paste

1 clove garlic, finely chopped

1½ cups vegetable stock

1 onion, chopped

3 tablespoons dried red lentils

1 carrot, chopped

1 small parsnip or potato, chopped

1 celery stalk, chopped

1 teaspoon tomato paste

pepper, to taste

1. Heat the oil in a lidded, nonstick saucepan, add the curry paste and garlic, and stir over low heat for 1 minute.

2. Add the stock and stir to combine, then add the rest of the ingredients and bring to a simmer over medium–high heat.

3. Turn the heat down, cover with the lid, and cook for 40–50 minutes, or until the lentils are tender.

4. Transfer half of the soup to a food processor or blender and process until smooth. Return the soup to the pan and reheat gently. Season with pepper and serve.

1
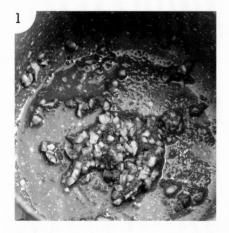

2

4

COOK'S NOTE
Use any leftover root vegetables in this soup—celeriac or sweet potato would be delicious.

Carrot & Cumin Soup

 SERVES 2    PREP TIME: 10 minutes    COOKING TIME: 30–35 minutes

nutritional information per serving	56 cal, 0.3g fat, 0.1g sat fat, 5.5g total sugars, 0.3g salt

This is one of the easiest low-fat recipes that you will find. No sautéing, just cook everything together and puree.

INGREDIENTS

1 carrot, finely chopped

1 clove garlic, chopped

1 shallot, finely chopped

1 ripe tomato, skinned and chopped

½ teaspoon ground cumin

1 cup vegetable stock

1 bouquet garni (sprigs of parsley, a bay leaf, and thyme tied together)

2 teaspoons dry sherry (optional)

salt and pepper, to taste

pinch of cumin and 1 tablespoon crème fraîche or Greek yogurt, to garnish

1. Put all the ingredients, except the sherry, in a large saucepan. Bring to a boil, then reduce the heat and simmer for 30 minutes, or until the vegetables are tender. Let cool slightly and remove the bouquet garni.

2. Transfer to a food processor or blender, in batches if necessary, and process until smooth.

3. Return to the saucepan, add the sherry, if using, and reheat gently. Taste and adjust the seasoning, if necessary. Remove from the heat and ladle into warm bowls. Garnish with cumin and a swirl of crème fraîche or Greek yogurt, and serve immediately.

1

1

2

COOK'S NOTE
To make your bouquet garni, just tie your desired herbs with string or put in a cheese-cloth bag with whole peppercorns.

Turkey, Sage & Mushroom Soup

 SERVES 6    PREP TIME: 20 minutes    COOKING TIME: 1–1¼ hours

nutritional information per serving	421 cal, 15g fat, 15.3g sat fat, 2g total sugars, 0.7g salt

Bridging the gap between risotto and stroganoff, this soup is a really filling staple for dinner.

INGREDIENTS

3 tablespoons butter

1 onion, finely chopped

1 celery stalk, finely chopped

25 large fresh sage leaves, finely chopped

4 tablespoons all-purpose flour

5 cups chicken stock

½ cup brown rice

3½ cups sliced white button mushrooms

1½ cups diced, cooked turkey,

1 cup heavy cream

salt and pepper, to taste

sprigs of fresh sage, to garnish

freshly grated Parmesan cheese, to serve

1. Melt half the butter in a large saucepan over medium–low heat. Add the onion, celery, and sage and cook for 3–4 minutes, until the onion is softened, stirring frequently. Stir in the flour and continue cooking for 2 minutes.

2. Slowly add about one-quarter of the stock and stir well, scraping the bottom of the pan to mix in the flour. Pour in the remaining stock, stirring to combine completely, and bring just to a boil.

3. Stir in the rice and season with salt and pepper. Reduce the heat and simmer gently, partly covered, for about 30 minutes, until the rice is just tender, stirring occasionally.

4. Meanwhile, melt the remaining butter in a large skillet over medium heat. Add the mushrooms and season with salt and pepper. Cook for about 8 minutes, until they are golden brown, stirring occasionally at first, then more often after they start to brown. Add the mushrooms to the soup.

5. Add the turkey to the soup and stir in the cream. Continue simmering for about 10 minutes, until heated through. Taste and adjust the seasoning, if necessary. Ladle into serving bowls, garnish with sage, and serve with Parmesan cheese.

Mediterranean Fish Soup

 SERVES 4

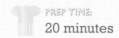 PREP TIME:
20 minutes

 COOKING TIME:
15–20 minutes

nutritional information per serving	361 cal, 6g fat, 1g sat fat, 5g total sugars, 2.7g salt

If you enjoy seafood, then this recipe is an absolute must. Not only is it quick to prepare but also the beautiful herby tomato garlic broth is a perfect carrier for the seafood.

INGREDIENTS

1 tablespoon olive oil

1 large onion, chopped

2 cloves garlic, finely chopped

2 cups fish stock

⅔ cup dry white wine

1 bay leaf

1 sprig each fresh thyme, rosemary, and oregano

1 pound firm white fish fillets (such as cod, red snapper, or halibut), skinned and cut into 1-inch cubes

1 pound fresh mussels, scrubbed and debearded

1 (14½-ounce) can diced tomatoes

8 ounces cooked, peeled shrimp, thawed if frozen

salt and pepper, to taste

fresh thyme sprigs, to garnish

crusty bread, to serve

1. Heat the oil in a large saucepan over medium heat and gently sauté the onion and garlic for 2–3 minutes, or until just softened. Discard any mussels with broken shells and any that refuse to close when tapped.

2. Pour in the stock and wine and bring to a boil. Tie the bay leaf and herbs together with clean string and add to the saucepan along with the fish and mussels. Stir well, cover, and simmer for 5 minutes.

3. Stir in the tomatoes and shrimp and continue to cook for an additional 3–4 minutes, or until piping hot and the fish is cooked through and flakes easily.

4. Discard the herbs and any mussels that have not opened. Season with salt and pepper, then ladle into warm bowls. Garnish with sprigs of fresh thyme and serve with crusty bread.

1

2

3

Broccoli Soup

 SERVES 6    PREP TIME: 10 minutes   COOKING TIME: 25–30 minutes

nutritional information per serving	104 cal, 0.7g fat, 0.1g sat fat, 1.5g total sugars, 0.5g salt

With few ingredients this soup is quick to whip up and ideal for using any leftover vegetables in the refrigerator.

INGREDIENTS

½ head of broccoli
1 leek, sliced
1 celery stalk, sliced
1 clove garlic, crushed
3 Yukon gold, red-skinnned, or white round potato, diced
4 cups vegetable stock
1 bay leaf
pepper, to taste
toasted croutons, to serve

1. Cut the broccoli into florets and set aside. Cut the thicker broccoli stems into ½-inch dice and put into a large saucepan with the leek, celery, garlic, potato, stock, and bay leaf. Bring to a boil, then reduce the heat, cover, and simmer for 15 minutes.

2. Add the broccoli florets to the soup and return to a boil. Reduce the heat, cover, and simmer for an additional 3–5 minutes, or until the potato and broccoli stems are tender.

3. Remove from the heat and let the soup cool slightly. Remove and discard the bay leaf. Transfer to a food processor or blender, in batches if necessary, and process until smooth.

4. Return the soup to the saucepan and heat through thoroughly. Season with pepper. Ladle the soup into warm bowls and serve immediately with crusty bread or toasted croutons.

1

2

3

GOES WELL WITH
A spoonful of crème fraîche or Greek yogurt is perfect for cutting through the soup with a slightly acidic tang.

Pea, Mint & Bean Soup

 SERVES 4

 PREP TIME:
10 minutes

 COOKING TIME:
25–30 minutes

nutritional information
per serving
221 cal, 5g fat, 1g sat fat, 4g total sugars, 1.5g salt

*If you want a good pantry standby, keep this recipe
in mind—it has a short list of simple ingredients and
doesn't take long to make, meaning it's ideal to make
with little fuss for a tasty and filling lunch.*

INGREDIENTS

1½ tablespoons olive oil

1 bunch scallions, trimmed and chopped

1 celery stalk, chopped

1 clove garlic, crushed

1 Yukon gold, red-skinned, or white round potato, diced

5 cups vegetable stock

1 bay leaf

1 cup peas

1 (15-ounce) can great Northern beans, drained and rinsed

salt and pepper, to taste

finely shredded fresh mint, to garnish

multigrain bread rolls, to serve

1. Heat the oil in a large saucepan over medium–high heat. Add the scallions, celery, and garlic and cook, stirring, for about 3 minutes, or until soft. Add the potato and stir for an additional minute.

2. Add the stock and bay leaf. Season with salt and pepper and bring to a boil, stirring. Reduce the heat to low, cover the pan, and simmer for 20 minutes, or until the potatoes are tender.

3. Add the peas and beans and return the soup to a boil. Reduce the heat, replace the lid, and continue to simmer until the peas are tender.

4. Remove and discard the bay leaf, then transfer the soup to a food processor or blender and process until smooth. Put a metal strainer over the rinsed-out pan and use a wooden spoon to push the soup through the strainer.

5. Reheat gently; do not boil. Ladle the soup into warm bowls, garnish with mint, and serve immediately with bread rolls.

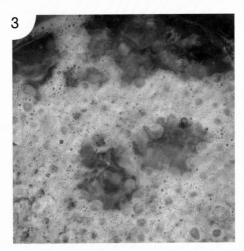

Fishermen's Soup

SERVES 6

PREP TIME:
10 minutes

COOKING TIME:
20–25 minutes

nutritional information per serving	333 cal, 20g fat, 3g sat fat, 4g total sugars, 0.3g salt

Use your own choice of firm white fish—teamed with crusty bread, this soup makes a quick, complete meal.

INGREDIENTS

2 pounds mixed white fish, such as cod, halibut, red snapper, and sea bass, and peeled shrimp

⅔ cup olive oil

2 large onions, sliced

2 stalks celery, thinly sliced

2 cloves garlic, chopped

⅔ cup white wine

4 tomatoes, chopped

pared rind of 1 orange

1 teaspoon chopped fresh thyme

2 tablespoons chopped fresh parsley

2 bay leaves

salt and pepper, to taste

lemon wedges, to serve

1. Cut the fish into large portions, discarding any skin. Heat the oil in a saucepan, add the onion, celery, and garlic, and sauté for 5 minutes, or until softened.

2. Add the fish and shrimp to the pan, then add the wine, tomatoes, orange rind, herbs, and bay leaf. Season with salt and pepper and add enough cold water to cover. Bring to a boil, then simmer, uncovered, for 15 minutes, or until the fish is cooked through and flakes easily.

3. Remove and discard the bay leaf. Ladle into warm bowls and serve immediately, with lemon wedges.

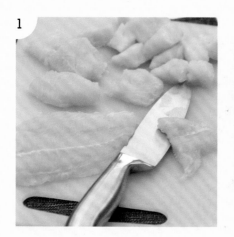

COOK'S NOTE
Use frozen prepared fish in this recipe for convenience and speed. Just be sure that it has thawed completely before adding to the pan.

Sweet Red Pepper & Tomato Soup

 SERVES 4   PREP TIME: 15 minutes    COOKING TIME: 30–35 minutes

nutritional information per serving	140 cal, 3g fat, 0.5g sat fat, 8.5g total sugars, 0.9g salt

This colorful soup is brimming with health-boosting vegetables and antioxidant-rich ingredients.

INGREDIENTS

1 tablespoon olive oil

2 tablespoons water

2 red bell peppers, seeded and finely chopped

1 clove garlic, finely chopped

1 onion, finely chopped

1 (14½-ounce) can diced tomatoes

5 cups vegetable stock

salt and pepper, to taste

fresh basil leaves, to garnish

1. Put the oil, water, bell peppers, garlic, and onion in a saucepan, heat gently, and cook for 5–10 minutes, or until the vegetables have softened. Cover the pan and simmer for an additional 10 minutes.

2. Add the tomatoes and stock, season with salt and pepper, and simmer, uncovered, for 15 minutes.

3. Serve garnished with basil leaves.

COOK'S NOTE To save time, use roasted peppers from a jar.

Provençal Turkey Soup

 SERVES 4

 PREP TIME:
15 minutes

 COOKING TIME:
45–50 minutes

nutritional information per serving	300 cal, 5g fat, 1g sat fat, 10g total sugars, 0.9g salt

Turkey is known for its low-fat qualities, but the base of this soup also lends itself well to chicken or shrimp, if preferred.

INGREDIENTS

1 tablespoon olive oil

2 red, yellow, or green bell peppers, seeded and finely chopped

1 celery stalk, thinly sliced

1 large onion, finely chopped

½ cup white wine

1 (14½-ounce) can plum tomatoes

3–4 cloves garlic, finely chopped

4 cups chicken stock

¼ teaspoon dried thyme

1 bay leaf

2 zucchini, finely diced

2½ cups diced, cooked turkey

salt and pepper, to taste

fresh basil leaves, to garnish

1. Heat the oil in a large saucepan over medium heat. Add the bell peppers, celery, and onion and cook for about 8 minutes, until soft and just beginning to brown.

2. Add the wine and simmer for 1 minute. Add the tomatoes and garlic.

3. Stir in the stock. Add the thyme and bay leaf, season with salt and pepper, and bring to a boil. Reduce the heat, cover, and simmer for about 25 minutes, or until the vegetables are tender.

4. Add the zucchini and turkey. Continue cooking for an additional 10–15 minutes, or until the zucchini are completely tender. Remove and discard the bay leaf.

5. Ladle into warm bowls, garnish with basil leaves, and serve immediately.

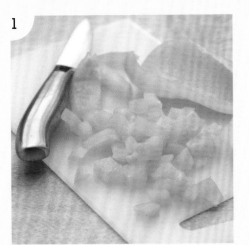

Chicken & Barley Broth

 SERVES 4 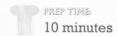 PREP TIME: 10 minutes 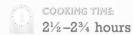 COOKING TIME: 2½–2¾ hours

nutritional information per serving	410 cal, 3.5g fat, 0.8g sat fat, 7g total sugars, 1.2g salt

This traditional hearty broth should be made two days ahead of serving—giving plenty of time for the flavors to soak into the barley.

INGREDIENTS

¼ cup presoaked dried peas
2 pounds lean chicken, diced
5 cups chicken stock
2½ cups water
¼ cup barley
1 large carrot, diced
1 small turnip, diced
1 large leek, thinly sliced
1 red onion, finely chopped
salt and white pepper, to taste
1 tablespoon chopped fresh parsley, to garnish
bread, to serve

1. Put the presoaked peas and diced chicken into a saucepan, then add the stock and water and bring slowly to a boil. Skim the stock as it boils. Wash the barley thoroughly and set aside.

2. When all the foam is removed, add the washed barley and a pinch of salt and simmer for 35 minutes.

3. Add the rest of the ingredients and simmer for 2 hours and skim again.

4. Let the broth stand for at least 48 hours. Reheat, season with salt and pepper, garnish with parsley, and serve with bread.

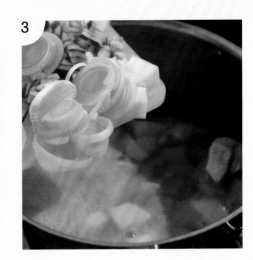

Russian Borscht *218*

French Onion Soup *220*

Tuscan Bean Soup *222*

Breton Fish Soup *224*

Caribbean Fish Chowder *226*

Paprika & Beef Soup *228*

Minestrone Soup *230*

Gazpacho *232*

Spicy Sausage & Bean Soup *234*

Chinese Pork & Potato Broth *236*

Irish Skink Soup *238*

Lamb & Vegetable Broth *240*

Vichyssoise *242*

Indian Potato & Pea Soup *244*

Spiced Lamb & Chickpea Soup *246*

Thai Shrimp & Scallop Soup *248*

Japanese-Style Beef Soup *250*

Wonton Soup *252*

Clam Chowder *254*

Corn Chowder *256*

Split Pea & Bacon Soup *258*

Curried Chicken Soup *260*

Miso Soup *262*

Vietnamese Crab Soup *264*

Around the World

Russian Borscht

 SERVES 6

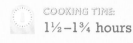 PREP TIME:
15 minutes
plus standing

COOKING TIME:
1½–1¾ hours

nutritional information per serving	252 cal, 10g fat, 6g sat fat, 22g total sugars, 1.1g salt

This sweet-and-sour soup based on beet and tomatoes and flavored with a fresh bouquet garni is popular in many Eastern and central European countries. It can be served hot or cold.

INGREDIENTS

5 raw beets (about 2¼ pounds)
5 tablespoons butter
2 onions, thinly sliced
3 carrots, thinly sliced
3 celery stalks, thinly sliced
6 tomatoes, peeled, seeded, and chopped
1 tablespoon red wine vinegar
1 tablespoon sugar
2 cloves garlic, finely chopped
1 bouquet garni (3 fresh parsley sprigs, 2 fresh thyme sprigs, and 1 bay leaf, tied together)
5½ cups vegetable stock
salt and pepper, to taste
sour cream, to serve
chopped fresh dill, to garnish

1. Peel and shred four of the beets. Melt the butter in a large saucepan. Add the onions and cook over low heat, stirring occasionally, for 5 minutes, until softened. Add the shredded beets, carrots, and celery and cook, stirring occasionally, for an additional 5 minutes.

2. Increase the heat to medium, add the tomatoes, vinegar, sugar, garlic, and bouquet garni, season with salt and pepper, and stir well, then pour in the stock and bring to a boil. Reduce the heat, cover, and simmer for 1¼ hours.

3. Meanwhile, peel and shred the remaining beet. Add it and any juices to the pan and simmer for an additional 10 minutes. Remove the pan from the heat and let stand for 10 minutes.

4. Remove and discard the bouquet garni. Ladle the soup into warm bowls and top each with a spoonful of sour cream, sprinkle with chopped dill, and serve immediately.

French Onion Soup

nutritional information per serving	480 cal, 23g fat, 11g sat fat, 7.5g total sugars, 2.2g salt

Traditionally, this is a soup served throughout the night to workers at the famous Les Halles market in Paris.

INGREDIENTS

6 onions (about 1½ pounds)

3 tablespoons olive oil

4 cloves garlic, 3 chopped and 1 kept whole

1 teaspoon sugar

2 teaspoons chopped fresh thyme, plus extra sprigs to garnish

2 tablespoons all-purpose flour

½ cup dry white wine

8½ cups vegetable stock

6 slices French bread

2½ cups shredded Gruyère cheese

1. Thinly slice the onions. Heat the oil in a large, heavy saucepan over medium–low heat, add the onions and cook, stirring occasionally, for 10 minutes, or until they are just beginning to brown. Stir in the chopped garlic, sugar, and chopped thyme, then reduce the heat and cook, stirring occasionally, for 30 minutes, or until the onions are golden brown.

2. Sprinkle in the flour and cook, stirring continuously, for 1–2 minutes. Stir in the wine. Gradually stir in the stock and bring to a boil, skimming off any foam that rises to the surface, then reduce the heat and simmer for 45 minutes. Meanwhile, preheat the broiler to medium–high. Toast the bread on both sides under the broiler, then rub the toast with the whole garlic clove.

3. Ladle the soup into six flameproof bowls set on a baking sheet. Float a piece of toast in each bowl and divide the shredded cheese among them. Place under the broiler for 2–3 minutes, or until the cheese has just melted. Garnish with thyme sprigs and serve at once.

1

2

3

French Onion Soup

 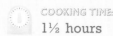
nutritional information **per serving**   480 cal, 23g fat, 11g sat fat, 7.5g total sugars, 2.2g salt

Traditionally, this is a soup served throughout the night to workers at the famous Les Halles market in Paris.

INGREDIENTS

6 onions (about 1½ pounds)

3 tablespoons olive oil

4 cloves garlic, 3 chopped and 1 kept whole

1 teaspoon sugar

2 teaspoons chopped fresh thyme, plus extra sprigs to garnish

2 tablespoons all-purpose flour

½ cup dry white wine

8½ cups vegetable stock

6 slices French bread

2½ cups shredded Gruyère cheese

1. Thinly slice the onions. Heat the oil in a large, heavy saucepan over medium–low heat, add the onions and cook, stirring occasionally, for 10 minutes, or until they are just beginning to brown. Stir in the chopped garlic, sugar, and chopped thyme, then reduce the heat and cook, stirring occasionally, for 30 minutes, or until the onions are golden brown.

2. Sprinkle in the flour and cook, stirring continuously, for 1–2 minutes. Stir in the wine. Gradually stir in the stock and bring to a boil, skimming off any foam that rises to the surface, then reduce the heat and simmer for 45 minutes. Meanwhile, preheat the broiler to medium–high. Toast the bread on both sides under the broiler, then rub the toast with the whole garlic clove.

3. Ladle the soup into six flameproof bowls set on a baking sheet. Float a piece of toast in each bowl and divide the shredded cheese among them. Place under the broiler for 2–3 minutes, or until the cheese has just melted. Garnish with thyme sprigs and serve at once.

Tuscan Bean Soup

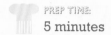 SERVES 6

 PREP TIME: 5 minutes

 COOKING TIME: 25–30 minutes

nutritional information per serving	270 cal, 8g fat, 1.5g sat fat, 0.5g total sugars, 0.3g salt

Here is a fantastic staples recipe that is ready in minutes, with virtually no preparation necessary.

INGREDIENTS

1¼ cups drained and rinsed canned cannellini beans

1¼ cups drained and rinsed canned cranberry beans

about 2½ cups chicken stock or vegetable stock

4 ounces dried soup pasta

¼ cup olive oil

2 garlic cloves, minced

3 tablespoons chopped fresh flat-leaf parsley

salt and pepper, to taste

1. Put half the cannellini beans and half the cranberry beans in a food processor or blender with half the stock and process until smooth. Pour into a large saucepan and add the remaining beans. Stir in enough of the remaining stock to achieve the desired consistency, then bring to a boil.

2. Add the pasta and return to a boil, then reduce the heat and cook for 15 minutes, or until just tender.

3. Meanwhile, heat 3 tablespoons of the oil in a small skillet. Add the garlic and cook, stirring continuously, for 2–3 minutes, or until golden. Stir the garlic into the soup with the parsley.

4. Season with salt and pepper and ladle into warm bowls. Drizzle with the remaining oil and serve immediately.

1

2

3

Breton Fish Soup

 SERVES 4

 PREP TIME:
20 minutes

 COOKING TIME:
40–50 minutes

nutritional information per serving	478 cal, 32g fat, 19.5g sat fat, 5.5g total sugars, 0.8g salt

The cider and sorrel provide a clean, fresh background flavor to the chunks of fresh fish in this French soup.

INGREDIENTS

2 teaspoons butter

1 large leek, thinly sliced

2 shallots, finely chopped

½ cup dry cider

1¼ cups fish stock

2 Yukon gold, red-skinnned, or white round potatoes, diced

1 bay leaf

¼ cup all-purpose flour

1 cup milk

1 cup heavy cream

2 cups fresh sorrel leaves (or spinach with a squeeze of lemon juice)

12 ounces skinless monkfish, red snapper, halibut, or cod fillet, cut into 1-inch pieces

salt and pepper, to taste

1. Melt the butter in a large saucepan over medium–low heat. Add the leek and shallots and cook for about 5 minutes, stirring frequently, or until they start to soften. Add the cider and bring to a boil.

2. Stir in the stock, potatoes, and bay leaf with a pinch of salt and bring back to a boil. Reduce the heat, cover, and cook gently for 10 minutes. Put the flour in a small bowl and slowly whisk in a few tablespoons of the milk to make a thick paste. Stir in a little more milk to make a smooth liquid.

3. Adjust the heat so the soup simmers gently. Stir in the flour mixture and cook, stirring frequently, for 5 minutes. Add the remaining milk and half of the cream. Continue cooking for about 10 minutes, or until the potatoes are tender.

4. Chop the sorrel finely and combine with the remaining cream.

5. Stir the sorrel cream into the soup and add the fish. Continue cooking, stirring occasionally, for about 3 minutes, or until the fish is cooked through. Season with salt and pepper, if necessary. Remove the bay leaf and serve immediately.

Caribbean Fish Chowder

 SERVES 4    PREP TIME: 15 minutes    COOKING TIME: 40–45 minutes

nutritional information per serving	360 cal, 16g fat, 5g sat fat, 7g total sugars, 1g salt

This is a chowder with a kick. Wonderful spices, chunks of fish, and sweet potato sitting in a creamy liquid makes a rich and tasty soup.

INGREDIENTS

1 pound red snapper fillets, skinned

3 tablespoons vegetable oil

1 teaspoon cumin seeds, crushed

1 teaspoon dried thyme or oregano

1 onion, diced

½ green bell pepper, seeded and diced

1 sweet potato, diced

2–3 fresh green chiles, seeded and minced

1 clove garlic, minced

4 cups chicken stock

¼ cup frozen peas

¼ cup frozen corn

½ cup light cream

salt and pepper, to taste

3 tablespoons chopped fresh cilantro, to garnish

1. Cut the snapper into bite-size chunks. Heat the oil with the cumin seeds and thyme in a large saucepan over medium heat. Add the onion, bell pepper, sweet potato, chiles, and garlic and cook, stirring continuously, for 1 minute.

2. Reduce the heat to medium–low, cover, and cook for 10 minutes, or until beginning to soften.

3. Pour in the stock and season with salt and pepper. Bring to a boil, then reduce the heat to medium–low, cover, and simmer for 20 minutes.

4. Add the fish, peas, corn, and cream. Cook over low heat, uncovered, for 7–10 minutes, or until the fish is just cooked; do not boil. Garnish with the cilantro and serve immediately.

Paprika & Beef Soup

 SERVES 8

 PREP TIME:
10 minutes

 COOKING TIME:
2–2¼ hours

nutritional information per serving	405 cal, 13g fat, 7g sat fat, 2g total sugars, 1.3g salt

A tradition German peasant-style soup, made with simple ingredients, makes a hearty and healthy complete meal.

INGREDIENTS

4 tablespoons butter

2¼ pounds boneless beef chuck or beef round, trimmed of fat and cut into ¾-inch cubes

10½ cups vegetable stock

2 onions, chopped

1 garlic clove, finely chopped

1 teaspoon paprika

¼ cup all-purpose flour

1 bouquet garni (3 fresh parsley sprigs, 2 fresh thyme sprigs, and 1 bay leaf, tied together)

3 Yukon gold, red-skinned, or white round potatoes, diced

salt and pepper, to taste

chopped fresh dill and shredded Gruyère cheese, to serve

1. Melt the butter in a large saucepan. Add the meat and cook over medium heat, stirring frequently, for 8–10 minutes, until lightly browned all over. Meanwhile, bring the stock to a boil in another saucepan.

2. Add the onions to the meat, reduce the heat, and cook, stirring frequently, for 5 minutes, until softened. Add the garlic and cook an additional 2 minutes. Stir in the paprika and flour and cook, stirring continuously, for 3–4 minutes.

3. Gradually stir in the hot stock and bring to a boil. Add the bouquet garni, season with salt, cover, and simmer, stirring occasionally, for 1 hour. Add the potatoes to the soup, replace the lid, and simmer for an additional 45 minutes, until the meat and vegetables are tender.

4. Remove the pan from the heat and taste and adjust the seasoning, if necessary. Remove and discard the bouquet garni. Ladle the soup into warm bowls, sprinkle with the dill and shredded cheese, and serve immediately.

  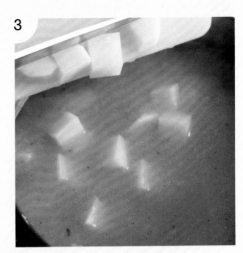

Minestrone Soup

 SERVES 4    PREP TIME: 20 minutes    COOKING TIME: 45–50 minutes

nutritional information per serving	352 cal, 9.5g fat, 2g sat fat, 12.5g total sugars, 1.8g salt

To Italians, "minestrone" means "big soup." It's a great way to use up leftover vegetables and make a wholesome meal big enough to feed a family.

INGREDIENTS

2 tablespoons olive oil

2 cloves garlic, chopped

2 red onions, chopped

3 ounces prosciutto, sliced

1 red bell pepper, seeded and chopped

1 orange bell pepper, seeded and chopped

1 (14½-ounce) can diced tomatoes

4 cups vegetable stock

1 celery stalk, chopped

1 (15-ounce) can cranberry beans, drained

1 cup shredded green cabbage

½ cup frozen peas

1 tablespoon chopped fresh parsley

3 ounces dried vermicelli pasta

salt and pepper, to taste

freshly grated Parmesan cheese, to serve

1. Heat the oil in a large saucepan. Add the garlic, onions, and prosciutto and cook over medium heat, stirring, for 3 minutes, until slightly softened.

2. Add the red bell pepper and orange bell pepper and the diced tomatoes and cook for an additional 2 minutes, stirring. Stir in the stock, then add the celery.

3. Add the beans to the pan with the cabbage, peas, and parsley. Season with salt and pepper. Bring to a boil, then reduce the heat and simmer for 30 minutes.

4. Add the pasta to the pan and cook according to the package directions, until tender but still firm to the bite. Remove from the heat and ladle into bowls. Sprinkle with Parmesan cheese and serve.

Gazpacho

 SERVES 4  PREP TIME: 25 mins plus chilling COOKING TIME: No cooking

nutritional information **per serving** 218 cal, 11.5g fat, 2g sat fat, 12g total sugars, 0.4g salt

Gazpacho has its roots in Andalucia, Spain and is a beautifully vibrant and deliciously refreshing soup, served chilled.

INGREDIENTS

1 red bell pepper, seeded and chopped

9 ripe tomatoes (about 2¼ pounds), peeled, seeded, and chopped

2 tablespoons minced onion

3 cloves garlic, crushed

1 cucumber, peeled and chopped

3½ slices stale bread, crumbled

3 tablespoons red wine vinegar or sherry vinegar

3½ tablespoons olive oil, plus extra for drizzling

1 cup ice cubes

salt and pepper, to taste

1. Set aside a handful of the red bell pepper, a handful of the tomatoes, and half the chopped onion in the refrigerator. Transfer the rest to a food processor or blender along with the garlic and cucumber and process until smooth.

2. Add the bread, vinegar, and oil and process again. Season with salt and pepper. If the soup is too thick, add the ice, then place in the refrigerator for 2 hours.

3. When ready to serve, season with salt and pepper, if necessary. Divide among serving bowls, sprinkle over the reserved red bell pepper, tomatoes, and onions, then drizzle a swirl of olive oil over the soup.

1

1

2

COOK'S NOTE
The soup is best
made during the
tomato growing
season, when
they will have
their best flavor.

Spicy Sausage & Bean Soup

 SERVES 6    PREP TIME: 15 minutes   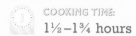 COOKING TIME: 1½–1¾ hours

nutritional information per serving	333 cal, 15g fat, 5.5g sat fat, 3g total sugars, 2.3g salt

This soup, also known as "fabada", has its origins in the Asturias region of Spain. It's simple, delicious, and full of flavor.

INGREDIENTS

7 cups vegetable stock

1 cup dried lima beans, soaked overnight in enough cold water to cover, rinsed and drained

1 cup dried cannellini beans, soaked overnight in enough water to cover, rinsed and drained

1 Spanish onion, chopped

2 cloves garlic, finely chopped

pinch of saffron threads

4 ounces morcilla or other blood sausage, sliced

2 chorizo sausages, sliced

4 bacon strips, diced

2 ounces smoked ham, diced

pinch of dried thyme

salt and pepper, to taste

1. Bring the stock to a boil in a large saucepan. Add the beans, onion, and garlic and bring back to a boil, then reduce the heat, cover, and simmer for 1 hour, until the beans are tender.

2. Meanwhile, put the saffron into a small bowl, add enough water to cover, and let soak.

3. Add the sausages, bacon, ham, thyme, and saffron with its soaking water to the pan, season with salt and pepper, and mix well. Replace the lid and let the soup simmer for an additional 30–35 minutes. Ladle into warm bowls and serve immediately.

Chinese Pork & Potato Broth

 SERVES 4

 PREP TIME:
20 minutes

 COOKING TIME:
30–40 minutes

nutritional information per serving	252 cal, 2.5g fat, 0.7g sat fat, 6g total sugars, 1g salt

Light and clean, this Chinese-influenced broth is quick to cook but full of zingy fresh flavors.

INGREDIENTS

4 cups chicken stock

2 large Yukon gold, red-skinned, or white round potatoes, diced

2 tablespoons Chinese rice wine vinegar

2 tablespoons cornstarch

¼ cup water

4 ounces pork tenderloin, sliced

1 tablespoon light soy sauce

1 teaspoon sesame oil

1 carrot, cut into thin strips

1 teaspoon chopped fresh ginger

3 scallions, thinly sliced

1 red bell pepper, seeded and sliced

1 (8-ounce) can bamboo shoots, drained

1. Put the stock, potatoes, and 1 tablespoon of the vinegar in a saucepan and bring to a boil. Reduce the heat until the stock is just simmering.

2. Mix the cornstarch with the water, then stir into the hot stock. Return the stock to a boil, stirring until thickened, then reduce the heat until it is just simmering again.

3. Put the pork slices in a dish and season with the remaining vinegar, the soy sauce, and sesame oil. Add the pork slices, carrot strips, and ginger to the stock and cook for 10 minutes. Stir in the scallions, bell pepper, and bamboo shoots. Cook for an additional 5 minutes. Ladle the soup into warm bowls and serve immediately.

Irish Skink Soup

 SERVES 4

 PREP TIME:
10 minutes

 COOKING TIME:
30–35 minutes

nutritional information per serving	251 cal, 11g fat, 6g sat fat, 10g total sugars, 0.7g salt

This version of Irish "Skink" is made with diced chicken and colorful summer vegetables, enriched with cream and egg yolk.

INGREDIENTS

2 celery stalks, halved lengthwise and diced

4 small carrots, thinly sliced

1 small leek, halved lengthwise and sliced

3½ cups chicken stock

1 bay leaf

1 cup diced, cooked chicken

½ cup shelled peas

4 small scallions, some green tops included, sliced

1 egg yolk

⅓ cup heavy cream

2 Boston lettuce, shredded

salt and pepper, to taste

1. Put the celery, carrots, and leek in a saucepan with the stock and bay leaf and season with salt and pepper. Cover and bring to a boil. Reduce the heat to medium, then simmer for 15 minutes, or until tender.

2. Add the chicken, peas, and scallions. Simmer for about 8 minutes, or until the peas are just tender.

3. Remove the pan from the heat. Lightly beat together the egg yolk and cream, and stir the mixture into the soup. Reheat gently, stirring.

4. Ladle into warm bowls, add the lettuce, and serve immediately.

Lamb & Vegetable Broth

 SERVES 8  PREP TIME:
15 minutes
plus chilling  COOKING TIME:
2–2¼ hours

nutritional information
per serving 250 cal, 13g fat, 6g sat fat, 8g total sugars, 0.2g salt

*This classic Scottish soup is simmered gently to let the
lamb, vegetables, and pearl barley become meltingly tender.*

INGREDIENTS

1½ pounds boneless
lamb shoulder

7 cups water

¼ cup pearl barley

2 onions, chopped

1 clove garlic, finely chopped

3 small turnips, diced

3 carrots, finely sliced

2 celery stalks, sliced

2 leeks, sliced

salt and pepper, to taste

2 tablespoons chopped fresh
parsley, to garnish

1. Cut the meat into small pieces, removing as much fat as possible.
Put into a large saucepan and cover with the water. Bring to a boil over
medium heat and skim off any foam that appears.

2. Add the pearl barley, reduce the heat, and cook gently, covered,
for 1 hour.

3. Add the onion, garlic, and vegetables and season with salt and
pepper. Continue to cook for an additional hour.

4. Remove the meat from the saucepan, using a slotted spoon.
Discard any fat or gristle. Put the meat back in the saucepan and let
cool thoroughly, then refrigerate overnight.

5. Scrape the solidified fat off the surface of the soup. Reheat, season
with salt and pepper, and ladle into bowls. Serve immediately,
garnished with the parsley.

GOES WELL WITH

Wedges of warm buttered soda bread are the perfect accompaniment for this hearty soup.

Vichyssoise

 SERVES 6

 PREP TIME: 40 minutes plus chilling

 COOKING TIME: 35–40 minutes

nutritional information per serving	310 cal, 22g fat, 13.5g sat fat, 8g total sugars, 0.3g salt

A really delicious chilled soup for summer entertaining but equally good served hot when the weather is chilly.

INGREDIENTS

5 leeks, white parts only

4 Yukon gold, red-skinned, or white round potatoes

4 tablespoons butter

5 cups water

2½ cups milk

1¼ cups sour cream, plus extra to garnish

salt and pepper, to taste

2 tablespoons snipped fresh chives, to garnish

1. Thinly slice the leeks. Peel and dice the potatoes. Melt the butter in a large, heavy saucepan over low heat. Add the leeks, cover, and cook, stirring occasionally, for 10 minutes.

2. Stir in the potatoes and cook over medium heat, stirring frequently, for 2 minutes. Pour in the water and add a pinch of salt. Bring to a boil, then reduce the heat and simmer for 15–20 minutes, until the potatoes are tender. Remove from the heat and let cool slightly.

3. Transfer to a blender or food processor and process until smooth. Push the mixture through a strainer into a clean saucepan with a wooden spoon, then stir in the milk. Season with salt and pepper and stir in half the sour cream.

4. Reheat the soup, then push through a strainer into a bowl. Stir in the remaining sour cream, cover with plastic wrap, and let cool. Chill in the refrigerator for 4–8 hours. Serve in chilled bowls, with swirls of sour cream and chives to garnish.

GOES WELL WITH

Wedges of warm buttered soda bread are the perfect accompaniment for this hearty soup.

Vichyssoise

 SERVES 6

 SERVES 6

 PREP TIME:
40 minutes
plus chilling

COOKING TIME:
35–40 minutes

nutritional information per serving	310 cal, 22g fat, 13.5g sat fat, 8g total sugars, 0.3g salt

A really delicious chilled soup for summer entertaining but equally good served hot when the weather is chilly.

INGREDIENTS

5 leeks, white parts only

4 Yukon gold, red-skinned, or white round potatoes

4 tablespoons butter

5 cups water

2½ cups milk

1¼ cups sour cream, plus extra to garnish

salt and pepper, to taste

2 tablespoons snipped fresh chives, to garnish

1. Thinly slice the leeks. Peel and dice the potatoes. Melt the butter in a large, heavy saucepan over low heat. Add the leeks, cover, and cook, stirring occasionally, for 10 minutes.

2. Stir in the potatoes and cook over medium heat, stirring frequently, for 2 minutes. Pour in the water and add a pinch of salt. Bring to a boil, then reduce the heat and simmer for 15–20 minutes, until the potatoes are tender. Remove from the heat and let cool slightly.

3. Transfer to a blender or food processor and process until smooth. Push the mixture through a strainer into a clean saucepan with a wooden spoon, then stir in the milk. Season with salt and pepper and stir in half the sour cream.

4. Reheat the soup, then push through a strainer into a bowl. Stir in the remaining sour cream, cover with plastic wrap, and let cool. Chill in the refrigerator for 4–8 hours. Serve in chilled bowls, with swirls of sour cream and chives to garnish.

1

2

3

FREEZING TIP
Freeze for up to three months. Defrost completely and stir well before serving cold or reheat gently.

Indian Potato & Pea Soup

 SERVES 4   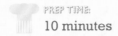 PREP TIME: 10 minutes    COOKING TIME: 30–35 minutes

nutritional information per serving	190 cal, 6.5g fat, 1g sat fat, 4g total sugars, 0.6g salt

A delicious mix of warming Indian spices and vegetables makes for a great filling lunch.

INGREDIENTS

2 tablespoons vegetable oil

2 white round potatoes, diced

1 large onion, chopped

2 cloves garlic, crushed

1 teaspoon garam masala

1 teaspoon ground coriander

1 teaspoon ground cumin

3½ cups vegetable stock

1 fresh red chile, seeded and chopped

⅔ cup frozen peas

¼ cup plain yogurt

salt and pepper, to taste

chopped fresh cilantro, to garnish

1. Heat the oil in a large saucepan. Add the potatoes, onion, and garlic and sauté over low heat, stirring continuously, for about 5 minutes. Add the garam masala, ground coriander, and cumin and cook, stirring continuously, for 1 minute.

2. Stir in the vegetable stock and red chile and bring the mixture to a boil. Reduce the heat, cover the pan, and simmer for 20 minutes, until the potatoes begin to break down.

3. Add the peas and cook for an additional 5 minutes. Stir in the yogurt and season with salt and pepper. Ladle into warm bowls, garnish with chopped fresh cilantro, and serve immediately.

TO SERVE *Poppadoms or naan are the obvious accompaniments.*

Spiced Lamb & Chickpea Soup

 SERVES 6   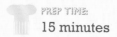 PREP TIME: 15 minutes    COOKING TIME: 2¾–3 hours

nutritional information per serving	330 cal, 8g fat, 2g sat fat, 6g total sugars, 0.8g salt

A classic Moroccan soup, traditionally eaten at Ramadan. As well as being healthy, it's crammed full of flavors, and the lentils and rice make it a hearty meal.

INGREDIENTS

2 tablespoons olive oil

8 ounces boneless lean lamb, cut into cubes

1 onion, chopped

⅔ cup dried chickpeas, soaked overnight, rinsed, and drained

6 cups vegetable stock

½ cup split red or yellow lentils

2 large tomatoes, peeled, seeded, and diced

1 red bell pepper, seeded and diced

1 tablespoon tomato paste

1 teaspoon sugar

1 teaspoon ground cinnamon

½ teaspoon ground turmeric

½ teaspoon ground ginger

1 tablespoon chopped fresh cilantro, plus extra to garnish

1 tablespoon chopped fresh parsley

¼ cup long-grain rice

salt and pepper, to taste

1. Heat the oil in a large saucepan. Add the lamb and cook over medium heat, stirring frequently, for 8–10 minutes, until lightly browned all over. Reduce the heat, add the onion, and cook, stirring frequently, for 5 minutes, until softened.

2. Increase the heat to medium, add the chickpeas, pour in the stock, and bring to a boil. Reduce the heat, cover, and simmer for 2 hours.

3. Stir in the lentils, tomatoes, red bell pepper, tomato paste, sugar, cinnamon, turmeric, ginger, cilantro, and parsley, and simmer for 15 minutes. Add the rice and simmer for an additional 15 minutes, until the rice is cooked and the lentils are tender.

4. Season with salt and pepper and remove the pan from the heat. Ladle the soup into warm bowls, sprinkle with cilantro, and serve immediately.

Thai Shrimp & Scallop Soup

 SERVES 4

 PREP TIME: 15 minutes

 COOKING TIME: 10–15 minutes

nutritional information **per serving**	128 cal, 1.5g fat, 0.3g sat fat, 1g total sugars, 2.7g salt

Quick to make, bursting with big flavors, yet clean and light to eat, this Thai broth makes a perfect palate-cleansing appetizer.

INGREDIENTS

4 cups fish stock

juice of ½ lime

2 tablespoons rice wine or sherry

1 leek, sliced

2 shallots, finely chopped

1 tablespoon grated fresh ginger

1 fresh red chile, seeded and finely chopped

8 ounces shrimp, peeled and deveined

8 ounces fresh scallops

1½ tablespoons chopped fresh flat-leaf parsley, plus extra to garnish

salt and pepper, to taste

1. Put the stock, lime juice, rice wine, leek, shallots, ginger, and chile in a large saucepan. Bring to a boil over high heat, then reduce the heat, cover, and simmer for 10 minutes.

2. Add the shrimp, scallops, and parsley. Season with salt and pepper and cook for an additional 1–2 minutes.

3. Remove the pan from the heat and ladle into warm bowls. Garnish with chopped parsley and serve immediately.

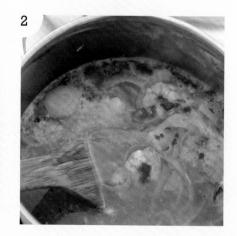

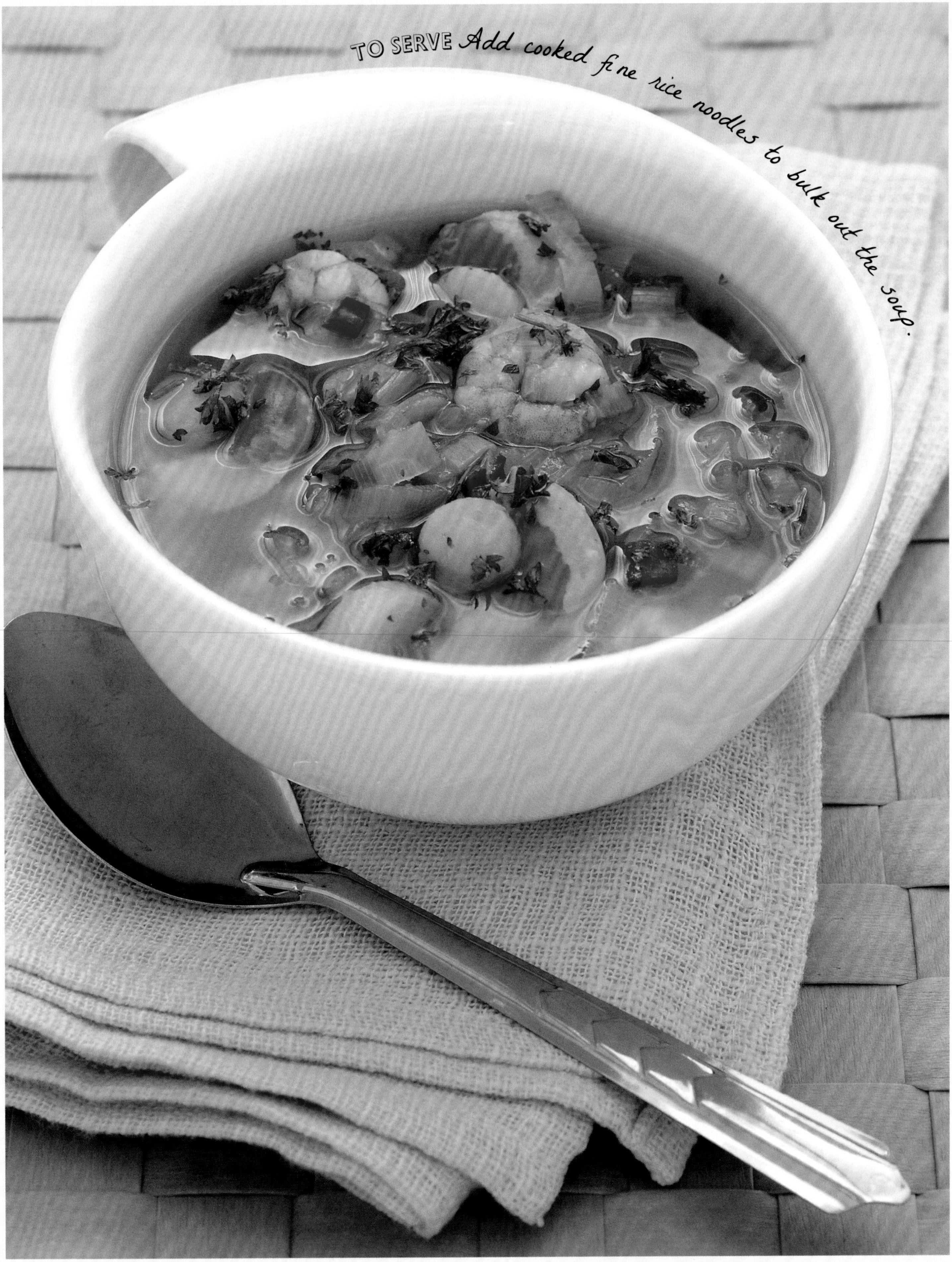

TO SERVE *Add cooked fine rice noodles to bulk out the soup.*

Japanese-Style Beef Soup

 SERVES 2    PREP TIME: 10 minutes    COOKING TIME: 15–20 minutes

nutritional information per serving	602 cal, 14.5g fat, 4g sat fat, 3.5g total sugars, 2.8g salt

If you want a warming, healthy, yet filling meal, look no farther than this miso-base noodle broth.

INGREDIENTS

4 ounces dried udon or soba noodles

2 tablespoons brown rice miso

2½ cups vegetable stock

1 tablespoon mirin or rice wine

5 baby corn, halved lengthwise

1 cup halved white button mushrooms

¾ cup bean sprouts

1½ cups baby spinach leaves

1 tablespoon peanut oil or sunflower oil

12 ounces thin top sirloin or tenderloin steak, cut into bite-size pieces

1 small red chile, thinly sliced

1. Cook the noodles according to the package directions, then drain and set aside.

2. Blend the miso with a little of the stock. Heat the remaining stock in a saucepan. Add the mirin, corn, and mushrooms and simmer for 3 minutes. Add the bean sprouts and simmer for an additional 1 minute. Remove from the heat and stir in the miso. Add the spinach and cover the pan.

3. Heat a wok or large skillet until hot. Add the oil and stir-fry the steak with the chile for 1–2 minutes, until browned, or cooked to your taste. Remove from the heat.

4. Pour boiling water over the noodles to reheat them. Drain well, then divide between two warm bowls. Ladle the miso-flavored soup and vegetables over the noodles. Top with the stir-fried beef and serve immediately.

1

2

3

COOK'S NOTE
This recipe calls for either udon or soba. Udon are the thicker wheat-base noodles; soba are thinner and made from buckwheat.

Wonton Soup

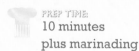 SERVES 6    PREP TIME: 10 minutes plus marinading    COOKING TIME: 5–10 minutes

nutritional information per serving	122 cal, 3g fat, 1g sat fat, 2g total sugars, 1.4g salt

The little Chinese packages are lightly poached in the soup broth to produce a tender finish.

INGREDIENTS

6 ounces ground pork or chicken

2 ounces peeled shrimp, ground

1 scallion, finely chopped

1 teaspoon finely chopped fresh ginger

1 teaspoon sugar

1 tablespoon Chinese rice wine or dry sherry

2 tablespoons light soy sauce

24 store-bought wonton wrappers

8½ cups vegetable stock

snipped fresh chives, to garnish

1. Mix together the pork, shrimp, scallion, ginger, sugar, rice wine, and half the soy sauce in a bowl until thoroughly combined. Cover and let marinate for 20 minutes.

2. Put 1 teaspoon of the mixture in the center of each wonton wrapper. Dampen the edges, fold corner to corner into a triangle, and press to seal, then seal together the two remaining corners.

3. Bring the stock to a boil in a large saucepan. Add the wontons and cook for 5 minutes. Stir in the remaining soy sauce and remove from the heat. Ladle the soup and wontons into warm bowls, sprinkle with snipped chives, and serve immediately.

1

2
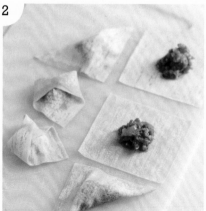

3

FREEZING TIP
Make the wonton packages in advance by following the first two steps. Then place on a lined baking sheet and put in the freezer. Once frozen, transfer to an airtight container and store for up to three months.

Clam Chowder

 SERVES 4  PREP TIME: 15 minutes  COOKING TIME: 25 minutes

nutritional information per serving	890 cal, 73g fat, 42g sat fat, 6.5g total sugars, 2.7g salt

Delicious classic New-England-style chowder, rich and creamy with a salty hit of bacon and thickened with potatoes.

INGREDIENTS

2 pounds fresh clams, scrubbed

4 bacon strips, chopped

2 tablespoons butter, plus extra for frying

1 onion, chopped

1 tablespoon chopped fresh thyme

1 Yukon gold or white round large potato, diced

1¼ cups milk

1 bay leaf

1½ cups heavy cream

1 tablespoon chopped fresh parsley

salt and pepper, to taste

1. Put the clams in a large saucepan with a splash of water. Cook over high heat for 3–4 minutes, until they open. Discard any that remain closed. Strain, reserving the cooking liquid. Let sit until cool enough to handle, reserving eight for the garnish.

2. Remove the clams from their shells, chopping them coarsely if large, and reserve.

3. In a clean saucepan, cook the bacon with a little butter until browned and crisp. Drain on paper towels. Add the butter to the same saucepan, and when it has melted, add the onion. Sauté for 4–5 minutes, until soft but not browned. Add the thyme and cook briefly before adding the diced potato, reserved clam cooking liquid, milk, and bay leaf. Bring to a boil, then reduce the heat and let simmer for 10 minutes, or until the potato is just tender.

4. Discard the bay leaf, then transfer to a food processor and process until smooth, or push through a strainer into a bowl.

5. Add the clams, bacon, and cream. Simmer for an additional 2–3 minutes, until heated through. Season with salt and pepper. Stir in the chopped parsley and serve, garnished with the reserved clams in their shells.

Corn Chowder

 SERVES 4  PREP TIME: 15 minutes  COOKING TIME: 30–35 minutes

nutritional information per serving	637 cal, 35g fat, 18g sat fat, 11.5g total sugars, 1.8g salt

This version of chowder uses fresh corn, so it's best made in the height of the corn season. Great for feeding a family, this soup is nutritious and hearty.

INGREDIENTS

6 ounces bacon, sliced into small pieces

2 tablespoons butter

1 large onion, chopped

1 bay leaf

5 fresh corn cobs (or 4 cups corn kernels)

2 cups milk

2 large cloves garlic, finely chopped

2 Yukon gold or white round potatoes, cut into small chunks

2 cups chicken stock

pinch of cayenne pepper

½ cup heavy cream

salt and pepper, to taste

3 tablespoons chopped fresh flat-leaf parsley, to garnish

1. Cook the bacon in a large, heavy saucepan for 5 minutes, or until starting to crisp. Add the butter and, once foaming, stir in the onion and bay leaf. Cover and cook over medium heat for 7–8 minutes, until the onion is soft but not browned.

2. Meanwhile, remove and discard the husks and silks from the corn cobs, then cut off the kernels using a small sharp knife. Put about two-thirds of the kernels in a blender or food processor with the milk and puree for at least 2 minutes, until smooth. Push through a fine strainer, discarding the solids left in the strainer and reserving the liquid.

3. Add the garlic and potatoes to the pan and moisten with a little of the stock. Add the cayenne pepper and season with salt and pepper. Cover and cook for an additional 5 minutes.

4. Pour the remaining stock and the reserved corn liquid into the pan and bring to a boil. Reduce the heat and simmer, partly covered, for 5 minutes.

5. Add the remaining corn kernels and cook for an additional 5 minutes. Stir in the cream and season with salt and pepper, if needed. Ladle into warm bowls, garnish with the parsley, and serve immediately.

Split Pea & Bacon Soup

 SERVES 6

 PREP TIME:
10 minutes

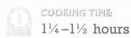 COOKING TIME:
1¼–1½ hours

nutritional information
per serving 280 cal, 15g fat, 6g sat fat, 4.5g total sugars, 2.4g salt

This thick and tasty soup, sometimes called "London Particular" is named after the so-called "peasouper" fogs that engulfed London in the first half of the last century.

INGREDIENTS

8 thick bacon slices

2 tablespoons butter

2 onions, chopped

2 carrots, chopped

2 celery stalks, chopped

⅔ cup dried yellow split peas, soaked in cold water for 1–2 hours and drained

7 cups vegetable stock

salt and pepper, to taste

croutons, to garnish

1. Dice 6 slices of the bacon. Melt the butter in a saucepan. Add the diced bacon and cook over low heat, stirring frequently, for 4–5 minutes. Add the onions, carrots, and celery and cook, stirring frequently, for an additional 5 minutes.

2. Increase the heat to medium, add the peas, pour in the stock, and bring to a boil. Reduce the heat, cover, and simmer for 1 hour.

3. Meanwhile, preheat the broiler. Broil the remaining bacon for 2–4 minutes on each side, until crisp, then remove from the heat. Let cool slightly, then crumble.

4. Remove the soup from the heat and season with salt and pepper. Ladle into warm bowls, garnish with the crumbled bacon and the croutons, and serve immediately.

1

2

3

Curried Chicken Soup

nutritional information per serving	224 cal, 9.5g fat, 5g sat fat, 8.5g total sugars, 0.8g salt

The traditional name for this soup, "mulligatawny" is derived from Tamil words for "pepper" and "water."

INGREDIENTS

4 tablespoons butter

2 onions, chopped

1 small turnip, cut into small dice

2 carrots, finely sliced

1 Pippin or Gala apple, cored, peeled, and chopped

2 tablespoons mild curry powder

5 cups chicken stock

juice of ½ lemon

1¼ cups bite-size cooked chicken pieces

2 tablespoons chopped fresh cilantro, plus extra to garnish

salt and pepper

½ cup cooked rice, to serve

1. Melt the butter in a large saucepan over medium heat, add the onions, and sauté gently for 5 minutes, until soft but not brown.

2. Add the turnip, carrots, and apple and continue to cook for an additional 3–4 minutes.

3. Stir in the curry powder until the vegetables are well coated, then pour in the stock. Bring to a boil, cover, and simmer for 45 minutes. Season with salt and pepper and add the lemon juice.

4. Remove the saucepan from the heat and let cool slightly. Transfer to a food processor or blender, in batches if necessary, and process to a puree. Return the soup to the rinsed-out pan, add the chicken and cilantro, and reheat gently; do not boil.

5. Put a spoonful of rice in each serving bowl and pour the soup over the top. Garnish with cilantro and serve immediately.

GOES WELL WITH
Some broken poppadoms sprinkled over the soup, and a minty raita, too.

Miso Soup

 SERVES 2  PREP TIME: 15 minutes  COOKING TIME: 5–10 minutes

nutritional information
per serving   154 cal, 7g fat, 0.8g sat fat, 1g total sugars, 2.7g salt

Miso is a highly nutritious staple in Japan, made from fermented soybeans. Together with barley or rice, it adds a unique umami-base flavor.

INGREDIENTS

4 cups water
2 teaspoons dashi granules
6 ounces silken tofu, drained and cut into small cubes
4 shiitake mushrooms, finely sliced
4 tablespoons miso paste
2 scallions, chopped

1. Put the water in a large saucepan with the dashi granules and bring to a boil. Add the tofu and mushrooms, reduce the heat, and let simmer for 3 minutes.

2. Stir in the miso paste and let simmer gently, stirring, until the miso has dissolved.

3. Add the scallions and serve immediately. If you let the soup sit, the miso will settle, so give the soup a thorough stir before serving to recombine.

1

2
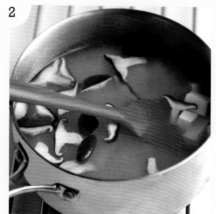

3
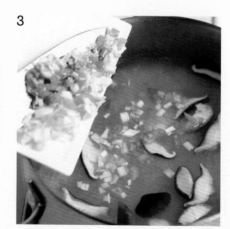

Vietnamese Crab Soup

 SERVES 6

 PREP TIME:
10 minutes
plus soaking

 COOKING TIME:
15–20 minutes

nutritional information per serving	288 cal, 11g fat, 1.5g sat fat, 1.5g total sugars, 2.6g salt

Light, clean, and fresh, this broth is quick and simple to make and perfect to kick off an Asian-style meal.

INGREDIENTS

6 dried shiitake mushrooms

1½ cups hot water

5 scallions

12 ounces asparagus spears, trimmed

1½ pounds white crabmeat, thawed if frozen

2 tablespoons peanut oil

3 cloves garlic, finely chopped

7 cups vegetable stock

1–2 tablespoons Thai fish sauce

3 tablespoons chopped fresh cilantro

1. Put the mushrooms into a bowl, pour in the water, and let soak for 20 minutes. Meanwhile, chop the white parts of the scallions and thinly slice the green parts diagonally. Slice the asparagus diagonally into ¾-inch pieces. Pick over the crabmeat and remove any pieces of shell and cartilage.

2. Drain the mushrooms, reserving the soaking liquid, and squeeze gently to remove the excess liquid. Remove and discard the stems and thinly slice the caps. Strain the soaking liquid through a cheesecloth-lined strainer.

3. Heat the oil in a large saucepan. Add the chopped scallions and garlic and stir-fry over medium heat for 2 minutes. Pour in the stock and reserved soaking liquid, add the mushrooms, and bring to a boil.

4. Stir in 1 tablespoon of the Thai fish sauce, add the sliced scallions and asparagus pieces, and bring back to a boil. Reduce the heat and simmer for 5 minutes, then gently stir in the crabmeat and cilantro. Simmer for an additional 3–4 minutes to heat through.

5. Remove the pan from the heat, taste, and stir in more fish sauce, if necessary. Ladle into warm bowls and serve immediately.

For Dunking &
Decorating

Pull-Apart White Loaf

 MAKES
1 loaf

 PREP TIME:
15 minutes
plus rising

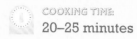 COOKING TIME:
20–25 minutes

nutritional information per loaf	1304 cal, 16g fat, 2.5g sat fat, 5g total sugars, 5g salt

This little loaf is designed to be torn, shared, and enjoyed fresh from the oven.

INGREDIENTS

1 teaspoon salt

2½ cups white bread flour, plus extra for dusting

1½ teaspoons instant yeast

1 cup warm water

1 tablespoon olive oil, plus extra for greasing

1. Put the salt in a mixing bowl and sift in the flour. Add the yeast and make a small well in the top. In a separate bowl, mix together the warm water and oil. Pour into the dry ingredients and mix to form a dough.

2. Knead the dough on a lightly oiled surface for about 10 minutes, or until you have a smooth, elastic texture. Alternatively, use a dough hook in a food processor and knead on a low setting for 5 minutes.

3. Transfer the dough to a lightly oiled bowl, cover, and set aside to rise in a warm place for about 1 hour, or until the dough has doubled in size.

4. Preheat the oven to 400°F and lightly dust a baking sheet with flour. Place the dough on the prepared baking sheet, then use a sharp knife to score a crisscross pattern in the top of the dough.

5. Bake in the preheated oven for 20–25 minutes, until golden brown. Transfer to a wire rack to cool.

Sage Tear & Share Bread

 MAKES
8 rolls

 PREP TIME:
15 minutes
plus rising

 COOKING TIME:
20–25 minutes

nutritional information per roll	192 cal, 5g fat, 0.7g sat fat, 1g total sugars, 0.6g salt

Baked as a single loaf, but served as individual rolls, this bread is the perfect side for a winter soup.

INGREDIENTS

1 teaspoon salt

2½ cups white bread flour

1½ teaspoons active dry yeast

1 cup warm water

3 tablespoons olive oil, plus extra for greasing

1 red onion, peeled and finely sliced

8–10 sage leaves, finely chopped

1. Put the salt in a mixing bowl and sift in the flour. Add the yeast and make a small well in the top. In a separate bowl mix together the warm water and 1 tablespoon of oil. Pour into the dry ingredients and mix to form a dough.

2. Knead the dough on a lightly oiled surface for about 10 minutes, or until you have a smooth, elastic texture. Alternatively, use a dough hook in a food processor and knead on a low setting for 5 minutes.

3. Transfer the dough to a lightly oiled bowl, cover, and set aside to rise in a warm place for about 1 hour, or until the dough has doubled in size.

4. Meanwhile, heat the remaining oil in a large saucepan over low heat. Add the onion and cook for 8–10 minutes, or until softened. Stir in the sage and remove from the heat. Knead the onion and sage mixture into the dough until evenly distributed, and the dough has returned to its original volume. Divide into 8 equal pieces and roll into balls.

5. Grease an 8-inch cake pan. Place the bread balls into the prepared pan, cover, and set aside to rise in a warm place for about 30 minutes. Preheat the oven to 400°F.

6. Bake in the preheated oven for 20–25 minutes, until golden. Transfer to a wire rack to cool.

1

4

4

Thyme, Red Onion & Olive Focaccia

 MAKES
1 loaf

PREP TIME:
30 minutes
plus rising

COOKING TIME:
30-35 minutes

nutritional information
per loaf

935 cal, 72g fat, 38g sat fat, 37g total sugars, 2.1g salt

This flat Italian-influenced bread is delicious with its sweet red onion, garlic, and olive topping.

INGREDIENTS

4 tablespoons butter

2 small red onions,
thinly sliced

4–5 sprigs thyme

3¼ cups white bread flour

2 teaspoons instant yeast

2 teaspoons granulated sugar

1½ cups lukewarm milk

2 eggs, beaten

1 clove garlic, finely chopped

10–12 ripe black olives,
pitted and halved

kosher salt, to taste

cracked black pepper, to taste

grated Parmesan cheese,
for sprinkling

1. Melt the butter in a small skillet over low heat and sauté the onion and thyme for 8–10 minutes, or until the onion is soft and caramelized. Remove from the heat and cool until required.

2. Grease a 10 x 14-inch baking sheet and line with parchment paper.

3. Sift the flour into a mixing bowl. Mix together the yeast, sugar, and milk in a small bowl and let stand at room temperature for 5–10 minutes, or until frothy. Mix in the eggs and pour into the flour. Mix to form a dough.

4. Transfer the dough to the prepared baking sheet, pushing it out to the edges. Cover and set aside to rise in a warm place for about 45 minutes, or until the dough has doubled in size. Meanwhile, preheat the oven to 350°F.

5. Spread the caramelized onion over the top of the bread and sprinkle with the garlic, olives, and Parmesan. Press the toppings lightly into the bread using your fingers. Season with salt and pepper.

6. Bake in the preheated oven for 30–35 minutes, until golden. Transfer to a wire rack to cool.

Mini French Baguettes

 MAKES
8 rolls

 PREP TIME:
15 minutes
plus rising

 COOKING TIME:
10–12 minutes

nutritional information per roll	171 cal, 2.7g fat, 0.5g sat fat, 0.6g total sugars, 0.9g salt

These are fun for children and adults alike and great for picnics or barbecues.

INGREDIENTS

1 teaspoon salt

2½ cups white bread flour, plus extra for dusting

1½ teaspoons active dry yeast

1 cup warm water

1 tablespoon olive oil, plus extra for greasing

1 egg yolk

1. Put the salt in a mixing bowl and sift in the flour. Add the yeast and make a small well in the top. In a separate bowl, mix together the warm water and oil. Pour into the dry ingredients and mix to form a dough.

2. Knead the dough on a lightly oiled surface for about 10 minutes, or until you have a smooth, elastic texture. Alternatively, use a dough hook in a food processor and knead on a low setting for 5 minutes.

3. Transfer the dough to a lightly oiled bowl, cover, and set aside to rise in a warm place for about 1 hour, or until the dough has doubled in size.

4. Knead the dough until it has returned to its original volume, then divide into eight equal pieces. Roll each piece out to a small rectangle shape and then roll up from the shortest side.

5. Lightly dust a baking sheet with flour and place the dough on the prepared baking sheet. Cover and set aside to rise in a warm place for about 45 minutes, or until the dough has doubled in size. Preheat the oven to 400°F.

6. Mix the egg yolk with 1 tablespoon of cold water and brush it over the loaves. Then use a sharp knife to score three lines in the top of each roll. Bake in the preheated oven for 10–12 minutes, until golden. Transfer to a wire rack to cool.

1

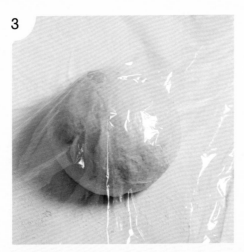

3

4

Ciabatta

 MAKES
2 loaves

 PREP TIME:
20 minutes
plus fermenting
and rising

 COOKING TIME:
20 minutes

nutritional information per loaf	787 cal, 9g fat, 1.6g sat fat, 4g total sugars, 4g salt

Ciabatta may not be quick to make, but the results are a full-flavored, light-textured crumb with a wonderful crisp crust. The recipe involves making a "starter" the day before cooking.

INGREDIENTS

½ teaspoon active dry yeast
2 tablespoons warm milk
⅔ cup warm water
1 tablespoon olive oil, plus extra for greasing
2 cups white bread flour, plus extra for dusting

starter

¼ teaspoon active dry yeast
⅓ cup plus 2 tablespoons warm water
1 cup white bread flour
1 teaspoon salt

1. To make the starter, mix together the yeast with 2 tablespoons of the warm water in a small bowl and let stand for 10 minutes. Put the remaining warm water, flour, and salt into a separate mixing bowl and gradually whisk in the yeast mixture until smooth. Cover and let stand overnight.

2. The next day, mix the yeast with the milk and let stand for 5 minutes.

3. Put the milk mixture, warm water, oil, flour, and starter mixture in a food processor fitted with a dough hook and knead for about 5 minutes. Transfer to a lightly oiled bowl, cover, and let rise in a warm place for about 1½ hours.

4. Line a baking sheet with parchment paper. Turn the dough onto a floured surface and cut in half. Shape each half of dough into an oblong about 10 inches long and place onto the prepared baking sheet. Cover and let rise in a warm place for about 2 hours.

5. Preheat the oven to 425°F. Dust the loaves with a little flour and bake at the bottom of the oven for about 20 minutes, until golden. Transfer to a wire rack to cool.

Potato Bread

 MAKES
8 slices

 PREP TIME:
10 minutes

 COOKING TIME:
45–50 minutes

nutritional information
per slice

170 cal, 9g fat, 5.5g sat fat, 0.6g total sugars, 0.17g salt

Potato bread is a popular accompaniment in many European countries, where potatoes are commonly used to make a filling for many kinds of dishes. This potato bread is a tasty alternative to traditional risen bread.

INGREDIENTS

4 russet potatoes
6 tablespoons butter, softened
¾ cup all-purpose flour
salt and pepper, to taste

1. Peel and coarsely chop the potatoes, then put in a saucepan of lightly salted cold water. Bring to a boil and simmer for 15–20 minutes, or until the potatoes are tender.

2. Meanwhile, preheat the oven to 375°F. Line a baking sheet with parchment paper. Drain the cooked potatoes and let cool slightly. Mash the potatoes using a ricer if you have one, then stir in the butter and flour and season with salt and pepper.

3. Place the potato mixture on the prepared sheet and roll out to about 10 inches square.

4. Bake in the preheated oven for 25–30 minutes, or until golden brown. Remove from the oven and cut into eight slices. Serve warm.

2

3

4

COOK'S NOTE

Preboil and mash the potatoes, then chill overnight and transfer to an airtight container and freeze for up to three months. Simply defrost to make the potato bread.

Garlic Focaccia

 MAKES
1 loaf

 **PREP TIME:**
15 minutes
plus rising

 **COOKING TIME:**
25–30 minutes

nutritional information per loaf	221 cal, 1.5g fat, 0.2g sat fat, 0.8g total sugars, 1g salt

A great bread to share with friends over a relaxed lunch or dinner. The origins of this flat bread are in Italy, where there are many regional variations, both sweet and savory.

INGREDIENTS

3 ⅔ cups white bread flour

1½ teaspoons active dry yeast

2 teaspoons sea salt

1¼ cups warm water

2 teaspoons olive oil plus extra for greasing

2 teaspoons fresh rosemary leaves, finely chopped

4 cloves garlic, thinly sliced

1. Put the flour, yeast, and 1 teaspoon of the salt in a mixing bowl and make a well in the top. In a separate bowl, mix together the warm water and 1 teaspoon of the oil. Pour into the dry ingredients and mix to form a dough.

2. Knead the dough on a lightly oiled surface for about 10 minutes, or until you have a smooth, elastic texture. Alternatively, use a dough hook in a food processor and knead on a low setting for 5 minutes.

3. Transfer the dough to a lightly oiled bowl, cover, and set aside to rise in a warm place for about 1 hour, or until the dough has doubled in size.

4. Line a baking sheet with parchment paper. Knead the dough until it has returned to its original volume. Transfer the dough onto the prepared baking sheet, pushing it out to the edges. Cover and set aside to rise in a warm place for about 1 hour.

5. Preheat the oven to 400°F. Spread the rosemary and garlic over the top of the bread. Press the toppings lightly into the bread using your fingers.

6. Bake in the preheated oven for about 20 minutes, until golden. Transfer to a wire rack to cool.

1

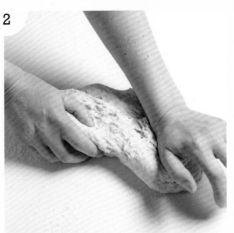

2

5

Cloverleaf Rolls

 MAKES
18 rolls

 PREP TIME:
15 minutes
plus rising

 COOKING TIME:
18–20 minutes

nutritional information per roll	106 cal, 1.6g fat, 0.2g sat fat, 0.4g total sugars, 0.44g salt

These pretty rolls are great for a celebration or special meal. The rolls are formed from three sections of dough, making them easy to tear apart. Try topping with different seeds, such as poppy or sesame, for variety.

INGREDIENTS

3⅔ cups white bread flour, plus extra for dusting

2 teaspoons salt

2 tablespoons olive oil, plus extra for greasing

1½ teaspoons active dry yeast

1¼ cups warm water

1. Put the flour in a mixing bowl with the salt, oil, and the yeast. Make a well and add the water. Mix to form a dough.

2. Knead on a lightly floured surface for about 10 minutes, or until you have a smooth, elastic texture. Alternatively, use a dough hook in a food processor on a low setting for about 5 minutes.

3. Put the dough in a lightly oiled bowl, cover, and set aside in a warm place to rise for about 1 hour, or until doubled in size.

4. Grease two 12-cup muffin pans with oil. Preheat the oven to 400°F.

5. Knead the dough until it has returned to its original volume. Divide into three equal pieces and then cut each one in half. Roll out each piece of dough to form a log about 6 inches long, then cut each log into three pieces. Divide each of these pieces into three and roll into small balls. You will have 54 balls of dough. Put three dough balls into each muffin cup, then cover and set aside in a warm place to rise for about 30 minutes, or until doubled in side.

6. Cook in the preheated oven for 18–20 minutes, until golden. Transfer to a wire rack to cool.

Garlic & Herb Dough Balls

MAKES
10 rolls

PREP TIME:
10 minutes

COOKING TIME:
12–15 minutes

nutritional information per roll	147 cal, 5g fat, 3g sat fat, 3g total sugars, 0.6g salt

These little dough rolls are yeast-free, and because there's no kneading or rising involved, they are quick and easy to make. They can be served as they are or tossed in the garlic and fresh herb butter. Serve as an accompaniment to soups and salads or with pizza.

INGREDIENTS

2¼ cups all-purpose flour
2¼ teaspoons baking powder
½ teaspoon salt
¾ cup milk
2 tablespoons maple syrup

garlic butter
1 clove garlic, crushed
1 tablespoon finely chopped flat-leaf parsley
4 tablespoons butter

1. Preheat the oven to 400°F and line a baking sheet with parchment paper. Sift the flour and baking powder into a bowl, add the salt, and make a well in the top.

2. Combine the milk and maple syrup in a separate bowl and pour into the flour. Mix to form a dough.

3. Shape the dough into 10 small circles. Place on the prepared baking sheet and baking in the preheated oven for 12–15 minutes, until golden brown.

4. To make the garlic butter, put all of the ingredients in a small saucepan and put over low heat until the butter is melted. Toss the warm rolls in the garlic butter and serve immediately.

COOK'S NOTE
As an alternative to oven cooking, put around the edge of a lightly oiled nonstick skillet and cook for about 10 minutes, until a crust has formed and the rolls are cooked through, turning regularly to prevent them from burning.

Potato Dumplings

 SERVES 4

 PREP TIME:
10 minutes

 COOKING TIME:
25—30 minutes

nutritional information **per serving**	290 cal, 2.5g fat, 0.5g sat fat, 1.5g total sugars, trace salt

These dense potato dumplings (or gnocchi) are a filling addition to soups, but can also be cooked in boiling water and served with herb butter.

INGREDIENTS

4 russet potatoes
1⅔ cups all-purpose flour, plus extra for dusting
1 egg, beaten
salt and pepper, to taste

1. Peel and cube the potatoes, and put in a saucepan of lightly salted cold water. Bring to a boil and simmer for 15–20 minutes, or until the potatoes are tender.

2. Drain the potatoes and mash using a ricer, if you have one. Put the mashed potatoes in a mixing bowl and add the flour and egg. Season with salt and pepper and mix to form a firm dough.

3. Knead on a lightly floured surface for about 1 minute, until the dough is smooth.

4. Divide the dough into four. Roll each piece into a log about 20 inches long. Then slice into 1-inch pieces and flatten each dumpling with the back of a fork. Repeat with the dough, placing the dumplings onto a lightly floured surface when complete. Set aside for 10–15 minutes before cooking.

5. To cook the dumplings, drop them into a saucepan of simmering soup—they are cooked when they rise to the top.

Italian-Style Bread Dumplings

 SERVES 4

 PREP TIME:
10 minutes
plus standing

COOKING TIME:
20 minutes

nutritional information
per serving

213 cal, 10g fat, 3.5g sat fat, 4g total sugars, 1.3g salt

These hearty little dumplings are perfect to help make a soup or stew a little more filling and are especially welcomed on a chilly winter evening.

INGREDIENTS

6 slices stale white bread

¾ cup milk

½ teaspoon olive oil

½ onion, minced

3 ounces smoked bacon, chopped

2 teaspoons finely chopped fresh flat leaf parsley

1 egg, beaten

1–2 teaspoons flour, for dusting

salt and pepper, to taste

1. Cut the crusts off the bread and discard. Cut the bread into small pieces and put in a bowl. Pour the milk over the bread, cover, and let stand.

2. Meanwhile heat the oil in a small skillet and sauté the onion and bacon for 5 minutes, or until the onion has softened.

3. Combine the cooked onion and bacon with the bread. Add the parsley and egg, season with salt and pepper, and let stand for an additional 15 minutes.

4. Form the mixture into about 16 small dumplings. Roll the completed dumplings lightly in flour to prevent them from sticking.

5. To cook the dumplings, drop them into a saucepan of simmering soup and cook for about 15 minutes.

Dim Sum Chicken Dumplings

 SERVES 4

 PREP TIME:
30 minutes

 COOKING TIME:
20–25 minutes

nutritional information per serving	158 cal, 3g fat, 0.8g sat fat, 2g total sugars, 0.9g salt

These dumplings are in the style of dim sum, traditional miniature Chinese snacks, and are a delicious addition to light soups and broths. Steam separately and then drop into the top of your soup bowls to serve.

INGREDIENTS

20–24 wonton wrappers

filling
2 skinless, boneless chicken breasts
½ bunch scallions, finely chopped
2 tablespoons chopped fresh cilantro
1 clove garlic, crushed
1 tablespoon soy sauce
1 tablespoon fresh ginger, peeled and grated
1 tablespoon rice wine vinegar
pepper, to taste

1. To make the filling, transfer all the ingredients to a food processor and process until everything is finely chopped.

2. Put 1 teaspoon of the filling mixture in the center of each wonton wrapper. Brush the edges of the wrapper with warm water and then gather two opposite edges and press together to form a seal. Repeat with the remaining two sides of the wrapper. Repeat until all the mixture is used.

3. To cook the dim sum, steam for 7–8 minutes, then drop into the soup to serve.

1

2

2

COOK'S NOTE
Instead of steaming, add to simmering stock and cook for 7-8 minutes, or until the chicken is cooked through, then serve in the cooking liquid as a light broth.

Crispy Pesto Croutons

 SERVES 4

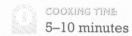 PREP TIME:
5 minutes

 COOKING TIME:
5–10 minutes

nutritional information per serving	211 cal, 10.5g fat, 1g sat fat, 1.5g total sugars, 0.7g salt

Croutons are not only a great way of using up leftover bread but also a fantastic standby ingredient that can liven up soups and salads. Try making a batch and keeping in the freezer or an airtight container.

INGREDIENTS

7 slices bread
2 tablespoons pesto sauce
(green or red, as preferred)
2 tablespoons olive oil
black pepper, to taste

1. Preheat the oven to 350°F and line a baking sheet with parchment paper. Remove and discard the crusts from the bread and cut the bread into cubes.

2. Put the pesto and oil in a bowl, season with the pepper, and whisk together well.

3. Toss the bread cubes in the pesto mixture and put on the prepared baking sheet. Bake in the preheated oven for 10–12 minutes, turning regularly, until golden.

4. Transfer to a wire rack to cool. Serve immediately, or transfer to an airtight container and freeze for up to three months.

1

2

3

SOMETHING DIFFERENT

Instead of pesto, add some finely chopped garlic and fresh or dried chopped herbs, such as rosemary. Or a touch of smoked paprika with a little oil.

Half & Half Loaf

 MAKES
1 loaf

 PREP TIME:
5 minutes
plus rising

 COOKING TIME:
30 minutes

nutritional information per loaf	1963 cal, 31g fat, 4.5g sat fat, 8g total sugars, 7g salt

Simply a 50:50 mix of white and whole-wheat flour, this is great for pleasing the whole family.

INGREDIENTS

2½ cups white bread flour, plus extra for dusting

1¼ cups whole-wheat bread flour

2¼ teaspoons active dry yeast

1½ teaspoons salt

1½ cups lukewarm water

2 tablespoons olive oil

vegetable oil, for greasing

1. Sift 1¾ cups of the white flour into a bowl, and mix the remainder with the whole-wheat flour in a separate bowl. Add half the yeast and half the salt to each bowl.

2. Make a well in the top of each bowl and add half the water and half the oil to each. Mix to form two doughs.

3. Turn out the doughs onto a lightly floured surface and knead separately for 10 minutes, or until you have a smooth, elastic texture. Return the doughs to the separate mixing bowls, cover, and set aside to rest for 5 minutes.

4. Grease a 9-inch loaf pan with oil. Turn out the doughs, shape each into a smooth circle and place one circle in each end of the prepared pan. Cover and set aside to rise in a warm place for about 1 hour, or until risen just above the top of the pan. Meanwhile, preheat the oven to 450°F.

5. Bake the loaf in the preheated oven for 5 minutes, then reduce the oven temperature to 400°F and bake for an additional 25–30 minutes, until golden brown. Transfer to a wire rack to cool.

Mixed Seed Bread

 MAKES
1 loaf

 **PREP TIME:**
15 minutes
plus rising

 **COOKING TIME:**
30–35 minutes

nutritional information per loaf	2163 cal, 38g fat, 5.5g sat fat, 31g total sugars, 7.5g salt

Made with a little rye flour and a mixture of seeds for extra flavor, this bread is nutty and delicious.

INGREDIENTS

2¾ cups white bread flour, plus extra for dusting

1 cup rye flour

1½ tablespoons instant nonfat milk

1½ teaspoons salt

1 tablespoon packed light brown sugar

1 teaspoon active dry yeast

1½ tablespoons sunflower oil, plus extra for greasing

2 teaspoons lemon juice

1¼ cups lukewarm water

1 teaspoon caraway seeds

½ teaspoon poppy seeds

½ teaspoon sesame seeds

topping
1 egg white, beaten with 1 tablespoon water

1 tablespoon sunflower seeds

1. Put the white flour, rye flour, instant milk, salt, sugar, and yeast in a mixing bowl. Pour in the oil and add the lemon juice and water. Stir in the seeds and mix to form a dough.

2. Knead the dough on a lightly floured surface for about 10 minutes, or until you have a smooth, elastic texture. Alternatively, use a dough hook in a food processor and knead on a low setting for 5 minutes.

3. Grease a bowl and a 9-inch loaf pan with oil. Transfer the dough to the oiled bowl, cover, and set aside to rise in a warm place for about 1 hour, or until the dough has doubled in size.

4. Turn the dough onto a lightly floured surface and knead for about 1 minute, or until smooth. Shape into a loaf the length of the pan and three times the width.

5. Fold the dough in three lengthwise and place in the pan with the seam underneath. Cover and set aside in a warm place to rise for 30 minutes, or until risen just above the top of the tin

6. Preheat the oven to 425°F. Brush the egg and water glaze over the loaf, then gently press the sunflower seeds all over the top.

7. Bake in the preheated oven for 30 minutes, or until golden. Transfer to a wire rack to cool.

1

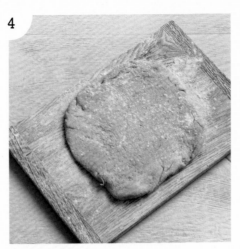

4

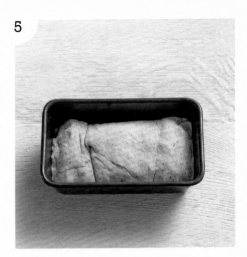

5

Garlic Spiral Rolls

 MAKES
12 rolls

 PREP TIME:
30 minutes
plus rising

 COOKING TIME:
25 minutes

nutritional information
per roll

222 cal, 9g fat, 4g sat fat, 0.5g total sugars, 0.7g salt

*A wonderful bread that's made for sharing, and packed
full of flavors to complement a winter soup.*

INGREDIENTS

3⅔ cups white bread flour,
plus extra for dusting

2¼ cups active dry yeast

1½ teaspoons salt

1½ cups lukewarm water

2 tablespoons oil,
plus extra for greasing

6 tablespoons butter,
melted and cooled

3 cloves garlic, crushed

2 tablespoons chopped
fresh parsley

2 tablespoons snipped
fresh chives

beaten egg, for glazing

sea salt, for sprinkling

1. Line a large baking sheet with parchment paper. Put the flour, yeast, and salt in a mixing bowl. Pour in the water and half the oil and mix to form a dough.

2. Knead the dough on a lightly floured surface for about 10 minutes, or until you have a smooth, elastic texture. Alternatively, use a dough hook in a food processor and knead on a low setting for 5 minutes.

3. Grease a bowl with oil. Transfer the dough to the bowl, cover, and set aside to rise in a warm place for about 1 hour, or until the dough has doubled in size.

4. Meanwhile, preheat the oven to 475°F.

5. Mix together the butter, garlic, herbs, and remaining oil. Roll out the dough to a 13- x 9-inch rectangle and spread the herb mix evenly over the dough to within ½ inch of the edge.

6. Roll up the dough from one long side and cut into 12 thick slices. Arrange, cut side down, on the prepared baking sheet about ¾ inch apart.

7. Cover and set aside to rise in a warm place for about 45 minutes, or until the dough has doubled in size. Brush with egg and sprinkle with sea salt. Bake in the preheated oven for 20–25 minutes, until golden. Transfer to a wire rack to cool.

Sunflower Twist

 MAKES
1 loaf

 PREP TIME:
10 minutes
plus rising

 COOKING TIME:
30–35 minutes

nutritional information per loaf	2472 cal, 78g fat, 10.5g sat fat, 19g total sugars, 7g salt

Full of flavor, this bread has a mild sweetness from the apple juice and a crisp topping of sunflower seeds.

INGREDIENTS

1½ teaspoons salt
1½ cups whole-wheat bread flour
2¼ cups white bread flour
2¼ teaspoons active dry yeast
1 cup lukewarm water
½ cup apple juice
1 tablespoon sunflower oil,
plus extra for greasing
¾ cup sunflower seeds
milk, for glazing

1. Put the salt and whole-wheat flour in a mixing bowl and sift in the white flour. Add the yeast and make a small well in the top. In a separate bowl, mix together the water, apple juice, and oil. Pour into the dry ingredients and mix to form a dough.

2. Knead the dough on a lightly oiled surface for about 10 minutes, or until you have a smooth, elastic texture. Alternatively, use a dough hook in a food processor and knead on a low setting for 5 minutes.

3. Transfer the dough to an oiled bowl, cover, and set aside to rise in a warm place for about 1 hour, or until the dough has doubled in size.

4. Grease a baking sheet with oil. Knead two-thirds of the sunflower seeds into the dough until it has returned to its original volume, then divide in half and shape into two logs about 10 inches long. Twist together the pieces of dough, firmly pinching the ends to seal.

5. Transfer the dough to the prepared baking sheet, cover, and set aside to rise in a warm place for about 1 hour. Preheat the oven to 450°F.

6. Brush the loaf with milk and sprinkle with the remaining sunflower seeds. Bake in the preheated oven for 10 minutes, then reduce the oven temperature to 425°F and bake for an additional 20–25 minutes, until golden. Transfer to a wire rack to cool.

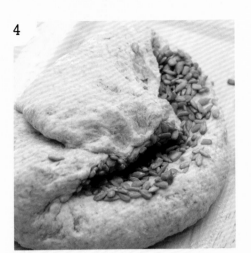

Parmesan Pull-Apart Loaf

 MAKES
2 loaves

 PREP TIME:
15 minutes
plus rising

 COOKING TIME:
15–20 minutes

nutritional information
per serving

959 cal, 12g fat, 3.5g sat fat, 5g total sugars, 4.2g salt

These beautiful little loaves are bound to be popular. They're best served warm and are perfect for serving at social gatherings, where everyone can pull off their own portion.

INGREDIENTS

3⅔ cups white bread flour
2 teaspoons salt
3 teaspoons extra virgin olive oil
2¼ teaspoons active dry yeast
1¼ cups warm water
1 tomato, thinly sliced
¼ cup grated Parmesan cheese

1. Put the flour in a mixing bowl with the salt, 2 teaspoons of the oil, and the yeast. Pour in the water and mix to form a dough.

2. Knead the dough on a lightly oiled surface for about 10 minutes, or until you have a smooth, elastic texture. Alternatively, use a dough hook in a food processor and knead on a low setting for 5 minutes.

3. Transfer the dough to an oiled bowl, cover, and set aside to rise in a warm place for about 45 minutes, or until the dough has doubled in size. Line two baking sheets with parchment paper.

4. Knead the dough until it has returned to its original volume, then divide in half and shape into two ovals. Transfer the dough to the prepared baking sheets, flatten the loaves, and sprinkle the tomatoes and Parmesan cheese over the tops. Cover and set aside to rise in a warm place for about 30 minutes. Preheat the oven to 400°F.

5. Drizzle the loaves with the remaining oil. Bake the bread in the preheated oven for 15–20 minutes, until golden brown. Transfer to a wire rack to cool.

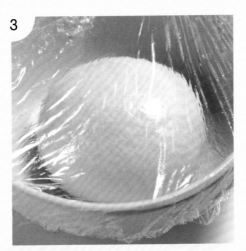

Chili Cornbread

 MAKES
10 slices

 PREP TIME:
10 minutes

 COOKING TIME:
25 minutes

nutritional information
per slice — 140 cal, 4.5g fat, 2g sat fat, 3g total sugars, 0.7g salt

Cornbread is quick and easy to make, and this recipe has a hot kick that cuts through creamy soups perfectly.

INGREDIENTS

1 cup all-purpose flour

1 cup cornmeal

1 tablespoon baking powder

½ teaspoon salt

¼ teaspoon crushed red pepper flakes

2 eggs, beaten

2 tablespoons melted butter

½ cup plain yogurt

2 tablespoons maple syrup

1. Preheat the oven to 400°F. Line an 8- x 11- inch cake pan with parchment paper.

2. Put the flour in a mixing bowl and stir in the cornmeal, baking powder, salt, and red pepper flakes. In a separate bowl, mix together the eggs, butter, yogurt, and maple syrup.

3. Pour the wet ingredients into the dry ingredients and stir until combined. Pour into the prepared cake pan and bake in the preheated oven for 25 minutes, until golden and a toothpick inserted into the bread comes out clean.

4. Remove from the oven and transfer to a wire rack to cool. Cut into 10 slices and serve.

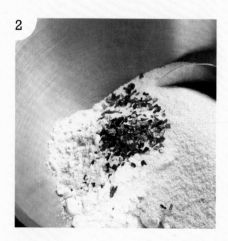

Poppy Seed Knots

 MAKES
16 rolls

 **PREP TIME:**
15 minutes
plus rising

 **COOKING TIME:**
18–20 minutes

nutritional information **per serving**	120 cal, 2g fat, 0.3g sat fat, 0.4g total sugars, 0.5g salt

These light, fluffy rolls are perfect served alongside soup. Simply smother with butter while still warm from the oven and enjoy.

INGREDIENTS

2 teaspoons salt

3⅔ cups white bread flour

1½ teaspoons active dry yeast

2 tablespoons olive oil, plus extra for greasing

1¼ cups warm water

1 teaspoon poppy seeds

1. Put the salt in a mixing bowl and sift in the flour. Add the yeast and make a small well in the top. Pour the oil and water into the dry ingredients and mix to form a dough.

2. Knead the dough on a lightly oiled surface for about 10 minutes, or until you have a smooth, elastic texture. Alternatively, use a dough hook in a food processor and knead on a low setting for 5 minutes.

3. Transfer the dough to an oiled bowl, cover, and set aside to rise in a warm place for about 45 minutes, or until the dough has doubled in size. Grease a baking sheet with oil.

4. Knead the dough until it has returned to its original volume, then divide into 16 pieces and roll each into an 8-inch-long log shape. Tie each log into a knot. Transfer the rolls to the prepared baking sheet, cover, and set aside to rise in a warm place for about 30 minutes. Meanwhile, preheat the oven to 400°F and lightly grease a baking sheet.

5. Sprinkle the poppy seeds over the rolls and bake in the preheated oven for 18–20 minutes, until golden. Transfer to a wire rack to cool.

Cheese Toasts

 MAKES
12 toasts

 PREP TIME:
5 minutes

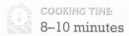 COOKING TIME:
8–10 minutes

nutritional information per 2 toasts	96 cal, 3.5g fat, 2g sat fat, 0.5g total sugars, 0.5g salt

These addictive cheesy croutons are simple to make and a real hit served with soups of all descriptions—plus they're the perfect way to use up day-old French bread.

INGREDIENTS

1 loaf French baguette

½ cup shredded cheddar, American, or Swiss cheese

1. Preheat the oven to 375°F.

2. Cut the baguette into about 12 slices and place on a baking sheet lined with parchment paper.

3. Sprinkle the cheese over the bread and cook for 8–10 minutes, until the cheese is just melted and golden.

2

3

3

Soda Bread

 MAKES
1 loaf

 PREP TIME:
15 minutes
plus resting

 COOKING TIME:
20–25 minutes

nutritional information per loaf	2016 cal, 98g fat, 31g sat fat, 25g total sugars, 8.6g salt

Soda bread is from the family of "quick breads"—baking soda reacts with buttermilk to create bubbles. The bread is best eaten on the day of making.

INGREDIENTS

2 tablespoons each fennel, poppy, sunflower, and pumpkin seeds

1 cup whole-wheat bread flour

1¾ cups white bread flour

3 tablespoons butter, plus extra for greasing

½ teaspoon granulated sugar

1 teaspoon baking soda

1⅓ cups buttermilk

1 teaspoon salt

1. Preheat the oven to 400°F and grease a baking sheet. Mix all the seeds together in a small dish.

2. Put the flours and butter in a mixing bowl. Rub in the butter until it resembles fine bread crumbs. Add the remaining ingredients and two-thirds of the seeds and mix to form a dough.

3. Place the dough on the prepared baking sheet, cover, and set aside to rest for 15 minutes. Use a sharp knife to score a cross in the top of the dough and sprinkle over the remaining seeds.

4. Bake in the preheated oven for 20–25 minutes, until golden. Transfer to a wire rack to cool.

2

3

3

SOMETHING
DIFFERENT
Create your own
blend of seeds—
you need a total
of ½ cup, but that
can consist of any
assortment.

Oyster Crackers

 MAKES
20 crackers

 PREP TIME:
15 minutes

 COOKING TIME:
40–45 minutes

nutritional information per cracker	30 cal, 0.5g fat, 0.3g sat fat, 0.1g total sugars, 0.13g salt

These small salted crackers (named for their shape, not ingredients) were originally intended to be served with oyster stews. They are the ideal accompaniment for soups because the little bite-size crackers stay crisp.

INGREDIENTS

1¼ cups all-purpose flour, plus extra for dusting
1 teaspoon instant yeast
½ teaspoon dried dill
½ teaspoon baking powder
½ teaspoon salt
2 teaspoons butter

1. Preheat the oven to 300°F and line a large baking sheet with parchment paper. Put the flour, yeast, dill, baking powder, and salt in a mixing bowl and set aside.

2. Put the butter and ½ cup of warm water in a small saucepan and put over low heat, until the butter is melted. Pour the butter mixture into the dry ingredients and mix to form a dough.

3. Lightly dust a surface with flour, then roll out the dough to about a ¼ inch thickness and use a 1-inch fluted cutter to cut out circles. Reroll the scraps and repeat until all the dough is used.

4. Place the dough circles on the prepared baking sheet and bake in the preheated oven for 40–45 minutes, or until golden brown.

5. Transfer to a wire rack to cool. Eat the same day or freeze in an airtight container for up to three months. If frozen, defrost and warm through for 5 minutes in a hot oven before serving.

Paprika & Chili
Toasted Seed Mix

 SERVES 6    PREP TIME: 5 minutes   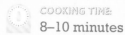 COOKING TIME: 8–10 minutes

nutritional information per serving	162 cal, 15g fat, 2.5g sat fat, 0.2g total sugars, 0.3g salt

These seeds are a great staples standby that can be made and stored in an airtight jar and used to top soups and stews. They are also perfect in salads.

INGREDIENTS

1 cup mixed seeds, such as pumpkin, sunflower, flaxseed, and sesame seeds

1 tablespoon extra virgin canola oil

½ teaspoon crushed red pepper flakes (optional)

½ teaspoon smoked paprika

½ teaspoon sea salt

1. Preheat the oven to 400°F and line a baking sheet with parchment paper.

2. Put all the ingredients in a bowl and toss well to combine. Sprinkle evenly onto the prepared baking sheet.

3. Roast in the oven for 8–10 minutes, stirring occasionally, making sure they don't burn.

4. Remove from the oven and let cool. Store in an airtight container for up to one month.

COOK'S NOTE

Swap the vegetable oil for sesame oil, and the paprika for soy sauce— roast the seeds as directed, then store in an airtight container, in a cool, dark place, for up to one week.

INDEX

COOK'S NOTE
Swap the vegetable oil for sesame oil, and the paprika for soy sauce— roast the seeds as directed, then store in an airtight container, in a cool, dark place, for up to one week.

INDEX